OSPREY COMBAT AIRCRAFT • 7

F-8 CRUSADER UNITS OF THE VIETNAM WAR

OSPREY
AVIATION

SERIES EDITOR: TONY HOLMES

OSPREY COMBAT AIRCRAFT • 7

F-8 CRUSADER UNITS OF THE VIETNAM WAR

Peter Mersky

Front cover

Nearly one half of all MiG kills scored by F-8 units were gained during CVW-21's 1967 deployment. In return the wing lost 23 aircraft and 18 pilots. On 19 May an escort of USS Bon Homme Richard (CVA-31) Crusaders launched to shepherd A-4s of VA-212 sent to bomb targets near Hanoi. The VF-24 F-8Cs would protect the Skyhawks, while F-8Es of VF-211 attacked various surface-to-air missile (SAM) sites and flak emplacements along the route.

As VF-24's Lt Phil Wood and flight leader Lt Bobby Lee approached their target, Lee called out a MiG. At first only he could see the enemy fighter, but eventually Wood spotted the MiG-17 saddling in on the tail of an A-6 Intruder from VA-35, which was also on the raid. Wood fired a Sidewinder missile but was too far away, the AIM-9 falling short of the target. Seeing the threat, the MiG pilot turned away, followed by Lt Wood in hot pursuit, who fired his Crusader's 20 mm cannon in two long bursts.

The sky was full of flak bursts and missile trails as the engagement wound its way towards Hanoi, the light grey puffs of 37 mm flak mingling with the darker grey of the 57 mm bursts and almost black puffs of the 85 mm shells. The SA-2 trails turned from white to pink in the bright sunlight and brilliant blue sky.

As he rejoined his flight, Wood quickly became aware of cannon fire hitting his fighter from behind – he was the target of another MiG-17, whose pilot had found himself in a solid position. Wood racked his F-8 into a left turn, desperately trying to throw off his pursuer's aim. He could see two other MiGs falling, and he later learned that one of them had been Lt Lee's victim. Wood's MiG was 1000 ft behind him as he held his stick hard left and punched in his afterburner.

Slowly, the MiG pilot lost his advantage as the American fighter came around, destroying the former's aim. He then tried to run for it, allowing Wood to come in behind and fire another Sidewinder – having launched with only three missiles, he was now down to just one AIM-9 on his upper right rail. But the second shot was enough. The MiG went down when the Sidewinder severed its T-tail from the fuselage, the enemy fighter pitching over and then falling towards the ground. Its pilot ejected. Although Wood flew close enough to his defeated adversary to see the patches on his flight suit, the North Vietnamese pilot did not survive the action for his parachute streamed and he fell to his death.

Unable to reach his own carrier, Lt Wood recovered aboard USS *Kitty Hawk* (CVA-63), where the crew of the A-6 he had rescued greeted him warmly. Upon inspection it was revealed that his F-8 (BuNo 147029 NP 443) had been so badly shot up that it was immediately grounded, never to fly again – the jet was eventually craned off the carrier in the Philippines upon the completion of CVA-63's on line period. Seventeen years later now Capt Phil Wood returned to *Kitty Hawk* as its commanding officer.

Iain Wyllie's specially-commissioned artwork shows Lt Wood just after achieving his MiG kill, bracketed by the intense flak and missile fire that characterised this engagement

Dedication

For Tim Hubbard and Dick Bellinger – MiG killers who've gone on before

First published in Great Britain in 1998 by Osprey Publishing
Michelin House, 81 Fulham Road, London SW3 6RB

ISBN 1 85532 724 4

Edited by Tony Holmes
Page design by TT Designs, T & S Truscott
Cover Artwork by Iain Wyllie
Aircraft Profiles by Tom Tullis
Figure Artwork by Mike Chappell
Scale Drawings by Mark Styling

Printed in Hong Kong

ACKNOWLEDGEMENTS

Besides the many F-8 'drivers' whose experiences are described herein, I would like to thank the following people for their help and support: Todd Baker and Roy Grossnick of the Naval Aviation History Office; Dr Ed Marolda of the Naval Historical Center; Daniel Crawford of the Marine Corps Historical Center; Don Montgomery of the Naval Media Center; Hill Goodspeed of the National Museum of Naval Aviation; Dave Donald of Aerospace Publishing; Angelo Collura of the Defense POW/MIA Office; Bill Northup; Dr Zoltan Buza; HMC(PJ) James Catrett; Mrs Johnnie Ann Hubbard; Mike O'Connor; Mrs Janie Conley; and Mrs Pat Vampatella.

CONTENTS

FIRST ENGAGEMENT

April 1965 – the war in South-East Asia was barely nine months old. Yet, except for the first reactionary raids following North Vietnamese PT-boat attacks in August 1964, and particularly the preceding February after a Communist attack on US barracks in Saigon, the area had been quiet. It was much like the 'Sitzkrieg', the 'Phoney War' of late 1939 and early 1940 when, after a flurry of fighting in Europe, the Germans had relaxed, lulling the Allies into a somnambulant state before the fall of Francek, and subsequent near-disaster at Dunkirk.

The only relatively constant activity, so far as the US aircraft carriers and their embarked squadrons were concerned, involved training flights, occasional reconnaissance sorties and the odd scramble to investigate a blip on a radarman's scope.

The growing influx of troops and supplies would soon become a flood. The 16,000 American advisors would eventually swell to more than half-a-million soldiers, sailors and Marines within five years. But in the early spring of 1965, bombing raids and even aerial encounters with the enemy were too few and far between to add up to any good O-Club stories.

The main concern was the constant stream of supplies sliding southward from North Vietnam down the circuitous Ho Chi Minh Trail. Some planners thought the solution to this problem required hitting this vast network of jungle trails, while others demanded strategic strikes at the head of the trail where the flood began – the 'North', especially its two major cities of Hanoi, the capital, and Haiphong, its nearby port city. These population centers were the hubs of the spiderwebs of railroads and rivers, the latter spanned by large bridges built mostly by the French.

The North Vietnamese were not oblivious to the strategic value of these tempting targets, and they had ringed many sites with impressive arrays of anti-aircraft artillery – AAA or flak, in the airman's vernacular.

On 3 April 1965, a strike group of Air Wing 21 (CVW-21) aircraft from USS *Hancock* (CVA-19) launched for a mission 'up north', four F-8Es from VF-211 escorting three A-4Es of VA-212 and three A-4Cs of VA-216. The aircraft would hit various railroad yards and bridges. The F-8s would attack the enemy flak sites, and each was loaded with 450 rounds of 20 mm cannon ammunition and eight Zuni rockets. The A-4s would try to hit the Dong Phong Thong Bridge, near the soon-to-be-famous Thanh Hoa Bridge. However, as the group neared the target area visibility decreased to about a mile in haze, mist and fog.

While a MiGCAP of F-4s from another carrier patrolled high above, the ten *Hancock* jets descended. Typically at this early stage of the war, there was little or no co-ordination between aircraft from different ships, resulting in the pilots of the F-8s and A-4s being totally unaware of the radio frequency their MiGCAP was on.

The Crusaders flew with the A-4s until the time came to 'punch' in afterburner, accelerate in front of the 'Scooters', and roll in on the flak sites that protected the bridge.

Three of the VF-211 Crusader 'drivers' were experienced, while an ensign flew wing on the flight leader. Lt Jerry Unruh and his wingman, Lt Bobby Hulse, followed Lt Cdr Spence Thomas and his new 'wingie' down as they dove toward the guns. The plan was to fire Zunis, then swing around for a strafing run with cannon, but the weather was not co-operating, and the first section quickly lost sight of the target after pulling off their first run.

Lt Cdr Thomas climbed to 10,000 ft as the A-4s tried their luck, but the Skyhawk pilots were also having trouble seeing their target. Now it was the second F-8 section's turn. The two Crusaders made their runs and pulled off, turning their attention to finding the new wingman, who was calling that he was lost. Using their radio's direction-finding capability, the senior Crusader aviators located the wayward 'nugget' just as Lt Cdr Thomas reported taking enemy fire.

At first, everyone thought they were over a flak site, but they soon realised that they were not alone in the air – the fire was coming from four North Vietnamese MiG-17s, the first time enemy fighters had appeared. While the flight leader had been orbiting at 10,000 ft, the MiGs had slid in from behind and started making runs on him.

Beset by the quartet of MiGs, Thomas hit his 'burner and blasted away from the 'swarm of hornets' he had attracted, whilst Lt Unruh dragged his flight of three Crusaders past the A-4s to rejoin his flight leader. Apparently, the MiGs had managed to 'mix' with the bomber flight during their pass at the ground targets. The lead F-8 was the only US Navy jet hit during the MiGs' fleeting pass, although Thomas's F-8E (BuNo 150845) had been badly damaged, taking cannon strikes in the canopy, wings and tail. The jet's utility hydraulic system was gone as well, preventing its pilot from raising the F-8's wing for a proper landing back aboard ship.

He therefore diverted to Da Nang where, after blowing down his landing gear with the emergency air system, he landed – Thomas was not injured, but his Crusader was a mess. The F-4 MiGCAP had not known the group they were supposed to be protecting was having problems! The rest of the *Hancock* strike group recovered safely.

Three senior naval aviators, each with more than 3000 hours in the Crusader and hundreds of combat missions over Vietnam, pose in 1987, some 20 years after their time at war. Jerry Unruh, David Morris and Bud Flagg (left to right) retired as flag officers, Unruh as a vice admiral and Morris and Flagg as rear admirals. Bud Flagg was *the* high-time F-8 driver with 3272 hours in all models

The four North Vietnamese MiG-17 pilots of the 921st Fighter Regiment who tangled with VF-211 Crusaders on 3 April 1965, claiming two F-8s, although all the Navy jets recovered. Left to right, Pham ngoc Lan, Phan van Tuc, Ho van Quy, and Tran minh Phuong (*via Dr Zoltan Buza*)

'The flight lead was never worried about himself over the target', now-retired Vice Adm Unruh observed years later. 'He was typical of the Crusader "drivers" at that time. He wanted to stay to protect the A-4s, and up to that point, the MiGs had never challenged us.'

Back at their base at Gia Lam, east of Hanoi, the MiG-17 pilots were proudly claiming two F-8s destroyed in this first aerial clash of the widening conflict. Pham ngoc Lan, Phan van Tac, Ho van Quy and Tran minh Phuong were members of the 921st 'Red Star' Regiment, the first North Vietnamese interceptor unit, which had been established little more than a year earlier. However, while the young MiG 'drivers' had certainly shaken up the American formation, their claims were erroneous for their target had recovered ashore, and having probably been claimed twice by the different Vietnamese People's Air Force (VPAF) pilots who thought they had shot down two different Crusaders.

It was not an auspicious beginning to the combat career of America's premier naval fighter, but in the coming four years the F-8 was to prove itself in several engagements with Communist MiGs, and in the larger war that would last nearly five more years, Vought's sleek jet would also show itself to be quite an 'earth-mover'.

SETTING THINGS UP

By the time of the so-called Gulf of Tonkin Incident in August 1964, Vought's F-8 Crusader was no stranger to the South China Sea, Navy and Marine Corps squadrons having operated in South-East Asia since 1961. That March, VMF-312 and VMF-154 had taken their 34 F8U-1Es (F-8Bs, after October 1962) to the Philippines to show the flag during a period of tension in Laos. In May of the following year, VMF-451 deployed eight of its Crusaders in *Hancock* to bolster the carrier's Navy air wing as it cruised the South China Sea during another crisis in Laos.

Navy carrier groups had been plying the waters off the Vietnamese coast for three years too. A-1 Skyraider pilots of various air wings had trained for inland bombing raids, and had even made a few actual attacks whenever the situation warranted. Further inland, naval aviators had been advising South Vietnamese pilots on flying newly-supplied examples of Douglas' sturdy, powerful, attack-bomber.

Six Navy AD-5Qs (EA-1Fs) of VAW-13's Detachment 1 from the carriers *Hancock* and *Coral Sea* (CVA-43) had also supplemented US Air Force efforts to counter Communist attempts at supplying their insurgent forces in South Vietnam by air.

Carrier-based Crusader units trained off Vietnam, but the only real combat runs had been by the RF-8A photo-Crusaders of VCP-63 and its descendent, VFP-63 –

Vietnam, 1967
(*Stephen D Oltmann, cartographer – courtesy Nautical and Aviation Publishing Company of America*)

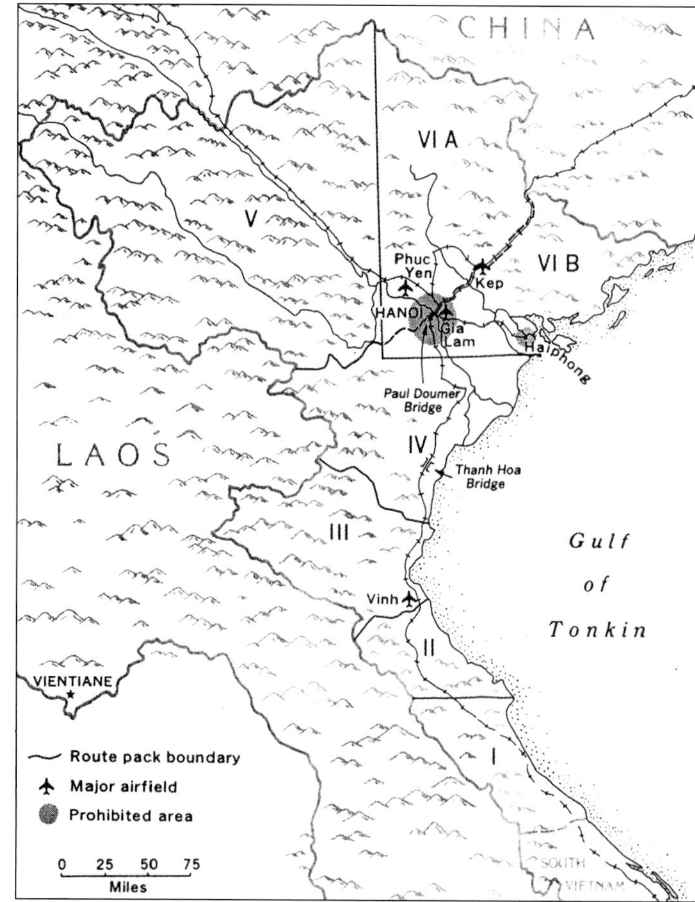

Route Packs and major bridges in North Vietnam, 1968
(Stephen D Oltmann, cartographer – courtesy Nautical and Aviation Publishing Company of America)

the careers of the RF-8A and RF-8G are discussed in depth in the companion Osprey Combat Aircraft volume *RF-8 Crusader Units in Cuba and Vietnam.*

The early Crusader units operating in South-East Asia were flying day fighter missions only, which meant exclusively engaging other enemy aircraft. Their load-carrying capabilities were limited to a somewhat comical speedbrake-mounted rocket pack. Besides, any Crusader 'jock' worth his gold wings blanched at the thought of cluttering up his thoroughbred with unsightly 'iron' bombs. It was enough that he had to carry Sidewinder air-to-air missiles against his cockpit canopy, but at least they were part of his air-to-air mission.

The F8U-2 (F-8C) arrived in 1958. It was instantly distinguishable from previous F-8s thanks to the prominent rear-fuselage ventral fins, which gave increased stability at high speed – the new fighter also sported a more powerful engine. The 'Charlie' was still strictly a day fighter, and increased the earlier two-Sidewinder load to four. The F8U-2N (F-8D) was originally intended to be a nightfighter, and both of these newer models could also tote four pods of Zuni air-to-ground rockets. The combination of the rocket pods and the F-8's four internal 20 mm cannon created a powerful ground-attack 'weapons system' suitable for knocking out flak sites and supply trains.

The 'Delta' had improved radar and avionics and still more engine power – many Crusader 'drivers' considered it to be the fastest of all the F-8s. It also offered the pilot a quantum improvement in engine control with the approach-power compensator (APC).

Like many new naval aircraft, the often-skittish F-8 had developed a reputation for being an 'ensign-killer' during its early service introduction, especially when landing aboard ship. The APC helped all F-8 pilots, but particularly junior aviators, during the tricky carrier approach, which was made all the more difficult in the Crusader due to the jet's relatively high approach speed of 147 knots. The APC assisted pilots in maintaining a consistent airspeed – the key to a good approach – by detecting changes in acceleration and angle of attack.

The 'Delta' also finally dispensed with the much-maligned, and seldom-used, ventral rocket pack featured in the earlier models.

The final development of the original F8U line, the F8U-2NE (F-8E) appeared in June 1961. Again offering upgraded avionics (mainly to fire the Bullpup air-to-ground missile, which was also seldom, if ever, used), the 'Echo' included a strengthened wing with two hard-points. For a long time the F-8E was the only Navy fighter capable of carrying the Mk 84 2000-lb bomb. The Marine Corps, in particular, was to make great use of the 'broad-shouldered' 'Echo' during the first half of the Vietnam War.

By mid-1964 Navy and Marine Corps Crusader squadrons were well-established and comfortable with the mounts, several units having already made deployments in carriers and to bases in Japan and the Philippines. The bugs had been largely worked out, and the early models that had served as trainers for the type's first years of service were gone, replaced by the models that would fight America's longest and in nearly every aspect, most debilitating and ultimately unsatisfying war. Even the way the conflict started was confusing . . .

By 1964 only two Atlantic-fleet fighter squadrons still flew F-8s, VF-13 and VF-62 usually being paired up in the same air wing. All other former F-8 AIRLANT fighter units were either transitioning to McDonnell's big, twin-engined, F-4 Phantom II, or had simply decommissioned. VF-13 and VF-62 would soldier on until they too decommissioned in 1969.

Several utility (VU) squadrons still operated various early model Crusaders into the early 1970s, and the Naval and Marine Corps Air Reserve also flew similar types in combined squadrons into the late 1960s, their F-8s carrying the somewhat ignominious label 'NAVY/MARINES' on their rear fuselages – the two separate organisations shared resources on different weekends.

The two replacement air group (RAG) squadrons – VF-124 at NAS Miramar and VF-174 at NAS Cecil Field – continued training newly-winged naval aviators and seasoned veterans returning to the fleet in the Crusader. However, VF-174 would be redesignated VA-174 in 1966 as the RAG for Vought's newest product, the A-7A Corsair II. VF-124 'Crusader College' thus became the only F-8 training squadron until it too changed aircraft types in 1970 when it began training Navy crews for

A division of 'Deltas' flies past *Coral Sea* in early 1964. Note the A-3 with its wings folded, right at the bow – its maintenance crew is probable doing some form of service on the big jet

the two-seat Grumman F-14A Tomcat, the latter jet considered to be the successor to the F-8 and, eventually, the F-4. In the mid-1960s, however, aspiring Crusader 'drivers' knew that action was to be had with any of the nine AIRPAC squadrons at Miramar.

At the time of the escalation of the Vietnam War, only two classes of carriers flew both the F-8 and RF-8, namely the four World War 2 vintage *Essex*-class carriers USS *Hancock*, USS *Bon Homme Richard* (CVA-31), USS *Oriskany* (CVA-34) and USS *Ticonderoga*, and the trio of so-called battle-carriers, USS *Midway* (CVA-41), USS *Franklin D Roosevelt* (CVA-42) and USS *Coral Sea* (CVA-43). The latter vessels were under construction when World War 2 ended, and they were duly mothballed, then resurrected, although none saw action during the Korean War of 1950-53. As with the surviving *Essex*-class carriers (which had been lumped into the 27C-class of US 'flattops' postwar), these ships had had their axial straight-decks altered to include an angled landing deck.

Throughout the Crusader's 30-year career of carrier operations, the three patches most prized by naval aviators were the Crusader shield-and-sword design, the circular 'Tonkin Gulf Yacht Club' patch and the somewhat later 'I Survived 27-Charlies in the F-8' patch. A fourth, rarer, F-8 patch, usually in blue, lamented, 'When You're Out of F-8s, You're Out of Fighters', and featured a stylised pilot with a prominent tear in one eye. It was a play on a beer commercial of the time, and called attention to the long, but assured, farewell the Navy was giving to its last single-seat fighter.

There was plenty of Crusader lore to entice neophyte fighter pilots into the community. Although barely 1300 Crusaders were eventually produced – including 144 photobirds, 42 F-8E(FN)s for France's *Aeronavale*, and a solitary two-seat F8U-1T (TF-8A) – the F-8's colourful early years and promise of the last single-seat, four-gun, action available to Navy and Marine Corps aviators, ensured that a steady stream of tough, competitive and usually capable fighter jocks flowed into the F-8 community even in the twilight of the jet's frontline career.

Ordnancemen load AIM-9 Sidewinders on a VF-51 F-8E aboard USS *Ticonderoga* (CVA-14) in February 1964

MAKING A WAR

When the French left their former colonies in Indochina in the late 1950s, the US stepped in to support the regimes that continued fighting a communist take-over. Sometimes, however, it seemed that the South Vietnamese leaders had little more to offer than the Hanoi-supported insurgents. Even frustrated members of the military occasionally rebelled, such as the two Vietnamese Air Force Skyraider pilots who strafed the Presidential Palace on 26 February 1962 – one was shot down.

On 1 November 1963 the government of Ngo Dinh Diem was toppled in a bloody coup in which Diem and his cohorts were killed. Three weeks later, America was in the midst of its own presidential agony following John F Kennedy's assassination in Dallas.

Recently declassified documents – including a memo written six weeks before he died – suggest Kennedy was leaning toward withdrawing American troops by 1965. President Lyndon B Johnson also considered pulling most advisors out of South Vietnam and leaving the South Vietnamese to fend for themselves. However, he froze all arrivals and departures until he and his advisors could sort things out in the wake of him becoming president following Kennedy's assassination.

How would history have gone if Johnson, a domestically-oriented president, had withdrawn from South-East Asia at this early stage? Events in the first half of 1964, culminating in action on the high seas, conspired otherwise, however. Johnson found himself in a major 'shooting' war, starting with build-ups and low-key patrols, but developing into full-scale American participation that, sociologically and politically, tore the country apart.

Combined activities involving all US services and those of South Vietnam included roving patrols along the Vietnamese coast, as well as alerts at airfields farther inland. Sometimes, these alert aircraft were called to respond to cries for help by Vietnamese ground units and their American advisors. These actions were meant to show the North Vietnamese that the South was not alone. The Navy's contribution to these actions was collectively called *Team Yankee*. Eventually, a geographic location in the South China Sea off South Vietnam was designated as a jumping off point and was dubbed 'Yankee Station'.

Laos was already a major 'hot spot' and was closely patrolled, photo-reconnaissance missions by Navy A-3 and RF-8 photo-aircraft mapping the *terra incognita* of the vast jungles of the area. Laos received its share of attention in 1963 and 1964 as the Navy confirmed the Communists were entering South Vietnam through the Laotian 'panhandle'.

At first, the 'recce birds' flew without escorts, although the crews of the RA-3s and RF-8s weren't too happy about going 'solo' over thickets of light AAA and small arms. However, on 6 June 1964 the situation changed dramatically when Lt Charles Klusmann of the VFP-63 det on

8 June 1964 – Cdr Doyle Lynn briefs Rear Adm William Bringle and Capt John F Butts (CO of *Kitty Hawk*) on his shootdown and rescue. The VF-111 CO was shot down and killed the following year while serving aboard USS *Midway* (CVA-41)

board *Kitty Hawk* was shot down during a photo run in eastern Laos. It was the first combat loss of a Crusader, and the second time in three days that Klusmann's aircraft had been badly hit. Unlike the earlier flight on 3 June when he had made it back to his ship, he had to eject from his burning aircraft. Klusmann was captured by Communist Pathet Lao forces and imprisoned for three months before he was able to escape. His full story is told in the companion RF-8 volume.

The following day, 7 June, another RF-8 flight launched in the early morning, followed by a second sortie later in the day. The main mission of the continued flights was to demonstrate American resolve after the loss of one of its aircraft and pilots. This time, however, the recce aircraft were escorted by fighter Crusaders. The first mission met with stiff defensive fire, and one of the escorts sustained minor damage.

Maintenance problems before the launch of the second mission caused one escort fighter to drop out, but three F-8Ds from VF-111, led by 'Sundowner' skipper Cdr Doyle W Lynn in BuNo 147064, did finally headed off toward the Plain of Jars in north-central Laos.

This group also encountered heavy flak, and Cdr Lynn's aircraft was fatally hit. He ejected, landing in a wood and watching as his friends circled forlornly overhead.

In a portent of things to come, and probably still hurting from its inability to retrieve Lt Klusmann the day before, the task force launched a massive rescue. Aircraft from the fleet offshore, supported by aircraft from Da Nang's alert pad, converged on Lynn's position. Using his survival radio and flares, the downed aviator was eventually able to signal a helicopter toward a clearing the next day. Lynn jumped aboard and was flown to Udorn, in Thailand, from where he eventually returned to his cheering squadron on board *Kitty Hawk*.

The Navy had learned a lot in three days. Specifically, not to underestimate the gunners on the ground, and how much effort would be involved in picking up crewmen from the thick jungle. It also learned (or rather had previous experiences in World War 2 and Korea reconfirmed) how vital the knowledge of such a rescue effort was to the men in the cockpits.

In a tragic sequel to these events, Cdr Lynn would be shot down again on 27 May 1965 flying VF-111 F-8D BuNo 148706 from the carrier *Midway* while on a raid to the southern North Vietnamese town of Vinh. This time, his luck ran out and he was killed in action.

ACTION IN THE TONKIN GULF

The Communist use of Laotian trails to infiltrate and resupply continued to be a problem, and the US became increasingly committed to bolstering the Laotians and South Vietnamese. Aircraft from several carriers and shore bases contributed to the surveillance missions of *Team Yankee*. With a break following the loss of the two Navy Crusaders from *Kitty Hawk*, recnce flights resumed on 14 June, with RF-8s from the newly-arrived USS *Constellation* (CVA-64) taking up the role. The *Ticonderoga* also arrived on 'Yankee Station' in July

The commanding officer of one of Air Wing 5's two F-8 squadrons on board *Tico* was thoughtful, aggressive, Cdr James Bond Stockdale. As an early Crusader pilot, he was the first to reach 1000 hours in Vought's world-beater, a feat he achieved while serving with VF-211 aboard *Midway* in 1959. Stockdale joined the 'Screaming Eagles' of VF-51 at Subic Bay, in the Philippines, in January 1963 as the unit's new executive officer, Cdr Arthur C 'Ace' O'Neal welcoming his new XO as *Tico* headed for the Tonkin Gulf.

The normal career path was for the XO to serve for 12 to 18 months then 'fleet up' to CO. It was both a finishing course for prospective skippers as well as a chance for the second-in-command to 'show his stuff' for the squadron he would soon lead.

Flying the new F-8E was challenging, but combined with the frustrating instructions from an increasingly indecisive administration in Washington (personified by the man who would become the ultimate political 'villain' of the Vietnam War, Secretary of Defense Robert S MacNamara), VF-51's deployment became a testing time for everyone. Washington kept a tight leash on the forces in the Gulf, especially the carrier aviators, who wanted desperately to go after the North Vietnamese whenever they could.

Jim Stockdale was never one to sit and wait. As he and his squadron orbited a ground battle during the summer of 1963, they watched for MiGs – a somewhat unnecessary task. At that stage the VPAF was poorly equipped, boasting only a few MiG-15s of Korean War vintage. The chances of engaging the VPAF were virtually non-existent, but Stockdale and his squadronmates did want to get into the fight. They knew they could help the embattled men on the ground.

'I saw these skirmishes down there', he said, 'the T-28s (powerful single-engine, two-seat trainers often used as armed light-attack aircraft in third-world countries) and ADs (pre-1962 designation for the Douglas AH-1 Skyraider) going against air-to-ground targets and troops. I said to myself, "If your CO cruise next summer is going to have any lasting meaning, you've got to get this squadron equipped for Zuni rockets".'

In his realistic, goal-oriented, manner, Cdr Stockdale looked for ways to better arm his squadron's Crusaders. Relieving Cdr O'Neil soon after returning to Miramar in July 1963, the new CO tasked his operations officer, Lt Cdr William Moore, who had flown ground-attack missions in F9F Panthers in Korea, with training VF-51 pilots in the use of the large rockets. Moore drew the air-to-ground kits, bombs and rockets and set up a programme for himself and five other pilots. These six would then train the rest of the squadron.

When *Tico* and her air wing deployed in April 1964, VF-51 was ready. Participating in the traditional operational readiness inspection (ORI), the final exercise-examination before deployment (it determined if units were, in fact, ready to perform whatever missions they might be called upon for), Stockdale's aviators proved they were ready for either their traditional air-to-air role or ground-attack with eight Zunis strapped to their Crusader 'Echoes'. The squadron's preparations would put them right in harm's way well before any of their compatriots in Air Wing 5.

After a port call at Sasebo, Japan, the *Tico* and her battle group arrived on 'Yankee Station'. A week later, as *Tico* made her way back to the Philippines, Cdr Stockdale was awakened with an urgent request to see the operations officer. Lt Cdr Moore had a Flash Top Secret message from Vice Adm Thomas Moorer, Commander Seventh Fleet – Moorer would later become Chief of Naval Operations.

The admiral wanted Stockdale and his unit (ten F-8s and pilots in all) to fly to the *Constellation*, now on 'Yankee Station'. A destroyer would pick up the groundcrew and transport them to the *Connie*. By mid-afternoon the transfer had been completed. It was 8 June 1964, and word was coming that Cdr Lynn had been rescued. *Kitty Hawk* was recovering the aircraft, some of which had been shot up during the rescue.

Admiral Moorer had heard about VF-51's unorthodox participation in the ORI's ground-attack exercises, and he knew that Stockdale's F-8s were the only Crusaders available to him capable of the ground-attack mission. *Constellation*'s two F-4B Phantom II squadrons, VF-142 and VF-143, had limited air-to-ground capability, not even internal guns. The Phantom IIs were duly 'sent to the beach' at Cubi to make room for more RF-8As that were coming out from the US to supplement the original photo-Crusaders. Besides *Constellation*, the carriers *Bon Homme Richard* and *Coral Sea* eventually operated combined photo dets that included Marine Corps aircraft and pilots.

For a month, VF-51 escorted photo-Crusaders, encountered flak, and occasionally attacked ground targets. Returning to *Ticonderoga* on 13 July, the 'Screaming Eagles' knew they had gained valuable experience.

By August 1964, intelligence reports indicated that the North Vietnamese were becoming increasingly nervous about the *DeSoto Patrols* being performed along their coast, as well as that of Communist China and North Korea. *DeSoto Patrols* were roving excursions begun in 1962 that were meant to probe defences and gauge the response from the target country. The *DeSoto Patrols* scheduled for early August promised to bring more than the usual attention from the North Vietnamese.

As USS *Maddox* (DD-731) steamed off the coast on the morning of 2 August 1964, the American destroyer's radar and lookouts picked out distant contacts. By mid-afternoon, three Soviet-made P-4 PT boats materialised in column. *Maddox* opened fire as the enemy boats closed, and the

VF-53 ordnance crewmen load their aircraft with Zuni rockets in mid-August 1964, just two weeks after the Gulf of Tonkin Incident. The Crusader is already spotted on the *Tico*'s No 1 catapult

Communist PTs returned the fire. The 20-minute fire-fight ended with all the P-4s damaged, while *Maddox* was hit by a single 14.5 mm round.

Ticonderoga F-8s from VF-51 and VF-53 answered the call for air support from the US destroyer. Cdr Stockdale and his wingman, Lt(jg) Dick Hastings, and VF-53 skipper Cdr Robair F Mohrhardt with his number two, Lt Cdr C Everett Southwick, attacked the retiring P-4s. The destroyer had by this time broken off its pursuit of the faster PTs.

Stockdale and Hastings each fired a Zuni, but both rockets missed. Mohrhardt and Southwick strafed the small craft with cannonfire, leaving one PT – T-339 – gushing smoke and eventually dead in the water. The VF-51 CO then joined his comrades in strafing passes.

Dick Hastings had been hit on his Zuni run, and Stockdale told him to orbit above the fight after checking his young wingman's F-8. Although there did not seem to be any leaking fluids, he could see that Hastings' fighter had a damaged right wing tip – no sense in taking chances this early in the game.

'I realised he had probably overstressed the aeroplane', Stockdale commented years later. 'He was on his first cruise, and this was the first live run made in the war. He tried to pull the wings off his Crusader. He didn't make any big mistakes. He could have thought he was on fire and ejected, but he didn't.'

The *Tico* F-8s had done the job – all three PTs were damaged, and the smoking P-4 finally sank. Now 350 miles from their carrier and at 'bingo' fuel (the point at which they had to break off the action because of low fuel), the four Crusaders rejoined. Not wanting to take any chances with the ability of his wingman's damaged aircraft to withstand the stresses of a recovery back aboard ship, Cdr Stockdale ordered Lt Hastings to land at Da Nang – Lt Dick Hastings was later killed when *Tico*'s LSO platform was struck by debris following a fatal landing accident by a VF-53 F-8E (BuNo 149176) on 30 November 1965. Grievously wounded in the crash, Hastings succumbed to his injuries a short time later.

The various actions centring around the PT boats had been the first direct combat between US forces and the North Vietnamese, who had made the point that they would not ignore what they considered as intrusions along *their* coasts, and were prepared to defend themselves. The Americans had also taken a stand – they would not be bullied from their support of their South Vietnamese allies, and were also ready to fight.

A day passed as both sides assessed the events of 2 August. USS *Turner Joy* (DD-951) joined *Maddox* as she resumed the interrupted patrol 48 hours after having been fired upon. The two ships headed back into the Gulf of Tonkin early on 4 August and cruised up and down the North Vietnamese coast all that day without much notice from the enemy. However, the Americans knew the North Vietnamese were preparing once again to do battle.

Before midnight, the destroyers' radars picked up fast-approaching contacts, lookouts identifying the bogies as more P-4s – probably from the same squadron that had attacked two days earlier. The PTs seemed to be headed for the *Ticonderoga* task group, and *Maddox* and *Turner Joy* soon opened fire at the speeding contacts, which then seemed to disappear astern of the destroyers. Thirty minutes later, more contacts 13 miles behind suggested another attack was imminent. Crewmen on deck and at their consoles reported what looked like a torpedo wake. Whatever it was, the destroyers steamed on at full alert.

Cdr Stockdale and two A-1 pilots from VA-52 arrived over the reported positions of the enemy boats and began strafing, although no one could see a target – Stockdale had launched solo after his wingman's Crusader went down with a generator failure. The best they could offer were sightings of ghostly wakes and bursts of light, which were perhaps gun flashes. Future four-star admiral, then-Cdr Wesley McDonald, CO of VA-56, was flying one of his A-4s above Stockdale. The VF-51 skipper had asked McDonald to radio *Maddox* and get the ship to flash its signal lights in order to give Stockdale a better idea of the ship's position.

Two hours after the initial contacts, quiet returned to the gulf, the targets on the radar scopes having vanished. However, more returned and the destroyers again found themselves under attack by PT boats. The ships fought a running battle until nearly 0100 on 5 August without any confirmed kills being achieved by either side.

Some – including Cdr Stockdale, who was certainly in a good position to see the action – doubted that the night engagements in the gulf had actually happened. In fact, when Robert McNamara visited Hanoi in November 1995, he asked Gen Vo Nguyen Giap (the leader of the North Vietnamese military establishment during the war) about the second so-called Gulf of Tonkin Incident. Giap laughed and shrugged, saying the attack had never occurred.

Whatever the truth regarding the two incidents in the Gulf of Tonkin, the Johnson administration in Washington decided that a retaliatory strike against the PT-boat bases and fuel farms was needed. Accordingly, Operation *Pierce Arrow* sent a 'one-time maximum effort attack' against the North Vietnamese on 5 August 1964. Sixty-seven aircraft from *Ticonderoga* and *Constellation* took part.

Tim Hubbard on a Crusader. He is wearing a tan flight suit, with green nylon G-suit and torso harness and brown flight boots. His white helmet carries red squares

Cdr Stockdale led the first strike, which included his six VF-51 Crusaders loaded with Zunis. The F-8s' targets were several AAA sites around the Vinh base. The A-4s and A-1s would hit other selected sites, including oil tanks and their defensive gun emplacements. Taking his flight of Crusaders down, Stockdale fired Zunis and cannon into the flak site. The other flights also hit their targets, and blasted out of the area. On the way out, Lt Tim Hubbard, flying wing on his CO, strafed an enemy PT boat on a river.

Although the raid was a success, and the target area was left in flames, two US aircraft were shot down by AAA, both from *Connie*'s Air Wing 14. Lt(jg) Richard C Sather from VA-145 crashed with his A-1H (BuNo 139760), becoming the first American naval aviator to die in Vietnam, whilst Lt(jg) Everett Alvarez of VA-144 ejected from his damaged A-4C Skyhawk (BuNo 149578 NK 411). Sather was killed, but Alvarez was captured and started his long eight-and-half-year stint as a PoW. A second strike involving VF-53's F-8s on the base at Quang Khe also met with some success.

One confounding aspect of the raid was the alert the North Vietnamese inadvertently received from no less a US official than the president himself. Lyndon Johnson told the American public about the events of the past three days, and what measures he was taking to respond. Unfortunately, as he addressed the nation on television, no one seemed to realise that the US raid would not launch for another two hours!

For the next few months, there was sporadic action in South-East Asia as far as naval aviation was concerned. Naval ships continued their patrols, and during this period of relative inactivity, the Communists – as they would during other lulls in the fighting in coming years – took advantage of the quiet to continue moving supplies south through Laos. By December, Washington was thoroughly frustrated with the lack of progress in curtailing such activities. The Johnson administration's hierarchy therefore planned two aerial campaigns – a series of strategic bombing raids against the north's industrial facilities, and armed recce missions to monitor the flow of material through Laos. These operations were called *Rolling Thunder* and *Barrel Roll*, respectively.

Navy and Marine Corps Crusader squadrons would be heavily involved in both these operations, especially as 1965 dawned.

WAR BEGINS IN ERNEST

Perhaps the USA, and the Johnson administration in particular, was surprised to find itself in a military build-up to an intense 'shooting' war. Certainly, there had been nothing like it since the summer of 1950 and the invasion of South Korea by the Communist north. A decade and a half is time enough to forget what war is like. Also, given that Lyndon Johnson desperately wanted to focus on building his so-called 'great society', with its concerns about economics and race relations, events beyond America's borders were nettlesome, and the big Texan resented having to deal with them.

Johnson had kept much of John Kennedy's cabinet, including Secretary of Defense Robert S McNamara and his 'whiz-kid' coterie of military illiterates. But as his television image stared into American living rooms that mid-summer's evening of 1964 to explain what the attacks in the Gulf of Tonkin meant, and what he intended to do about them, Lyndon Johnson was a frightened, unsure, chief executive who truly needed – but lacked – men of understanding and honour around him.

As December 1964 merged in January 1965, the American build-up in South Vietnam and in the South China Sea continued at a feverish pace. On the flip side, the North Vietnamese, and their minions, also kept the trucks moving toward the south. *Barrel Roll* missions occasionally caught the Communist trucks in the open, but even when the rebels attacked an American barracks in Saigon on Christmas Eve 1964, killing two Americans and injuring more than a hundred other nationals, Johnson did not escalate the conflict. The carriers off the coast – *Hancock*, *Coral Sea* and *Ranger* (CVA-61) - dutifully orbited on 'Yankee Station' awaiting orders.

On 13 January 1965 VF-24's Lt(jg) Tom Irwin returned from a day-time air-intercept training mission. Irwin snagged the carrier's 4-wire, and the rollout seemed normal. He was about to retard the throttle when he suddenly realised that he was not stopping – the F-8C (BuNo 147011) was headed for the edge. Irwin had to consider the two-second delay between selection and 'burner light.

VF-24 combat veteran Tom Irwin is seen standing by his RF-8G before a training mission from NAF Washington, DC, in 1978. With the rank of commander, Irwin led VFP-306 (one of two Naval Air Reserve VFP squadrons) in the late 1970s, and had also served as the OINC for the second squadron, VFP-206. He later attained flag rank as a reservist. Today, Irwin is in a senior management position with TWA

The young aviator could not know that his hook point had sheared from the shank. He selected 'burner, but the Crusader floated over the angle, the indicated airspeed below the 80 knots needed for a successful ejection – zero-airspeed-zero-altitude ejection seats had not yet arrived in the fleet. Irwin pulled the canopy jettison handle, but although the latches released, there was not enough airflow to carry the canopy away, and it stayed on the doomed fighter.

In the limited time remaining, he considered an out-of-the-envelope ejection, but decided to stay with the doomed jet. Irwin had enough airspeed for limited pitch control, at least until his main wheels rolled over the deck edge. By using the rudder to keep his wings level, he was able to enter the water more or less level, rather than nose first or in a cartwheel.

As the F-8 hit the water, the afterburner ignited, causing the engine to explode. The splash also carried away the canopy, and although the Crusader entered the water upright, water immediately began pouring over the cockpit sill. Irwin pulled the ditching handle, which released him from the seat, and he bobbed out of the cockpit just as a wave splashed over him.

Having returned home in the summer of 1965 after completing their first combat deployment, pilots from VF-24 visit with Adm Moore (COMNAVAIRPAC) in San Diego. The admiral has just presented the aviators with Air Medals. They are, from left to right; Adm Moore, Vince Furey, Harry Post (CO), Dave Benson, Fred Richardson, Greg Gregory, Cecil Tune, Dick Laws, Kent Billue, Norm Black, John Allen, Tom Irwin and Fred Neth. Lt Cdr Richardson was one of the few black aviators in jets at the time, and had previously flown F-3 Demons. Lt(jg) Laws was killed in action on the next cruise, whilst Lt Cdr Neth lost his life the following February in an operational mishap off *Hancock*

The oxygen hose from the seat pan to his mask was entangled on the canopy handle on the right canopy rail. While awash, and laying on the rail, Irwin separated the connector at the end of the mask hose and quickly rolled over the side of his fighter. The forward end of the centre section of the Crusader's two-position wing, and most of the vertical stabiliser, were all that remained above the water.

Having inflated his life preserver, Irwin swam away as his Crusader finally sank out of sight. The *Hancock* had stopped close to his position, and the ship's H-2 helicopter plucked him from the South China Sea. His jet had taken two seconds to reach the water after rolling off the deck, and it had taken two minutes to pluck him from the water and deposit him safely on the flightdeck. He noted later, 'I was never able to duplicate my emergency egress time from a cockpit onto a work stand in the hanger'.

Vought had initially installed its own ejection seat into the F-8, but had changed to a Martin-Baker seat, which had earned a good reputation in Britain. The latter's Mk 5 system did not have a zero-zero capability, but eventually the Mk F-7 zero-zero seat was installed in late-model F-8s.

As the build-up of American forces in South-East Asia began in earnest following the Gulf of Tonkin Incident, F-8s served in every carrier in the South China Sea, at least in the recce role, and in the case of the smaller 27C class and *Midway*-class carriers in the fighter role as well. While the larger ships included F-4B units as their primary fighter complement, the smaller decks made full use of the F-8's bomb-toting capabilities.

A Communist attack on American and South Vietnamese facilities in February 1965 finally brought an increased US response. VF-24's Lt(jg) Irwin participated in the 7 February 1965 strike – called *Flaming Dart* – into North Vietnam, followed four days later by another raid – *Flaming Dart II* – on the Chan Hoa barracks near Dong Hoi airfield. Here, he recalls the early days of the war;

'By the middle of March 1965, daily strikes had become routine. At this time the strikes were handled as ship-wide strikes, with one big one for the day. They had all the support elements – tankers, weather, recce, AEW, CAP – and, on occasion, flak suppression with Zunis.

'The CAP was armed with 400 rounds of 20 mm and two Sidewinders

7 February 1965 – an A-4E of VA-212 armed with rocket pods taxies toward the catapult aboard *Hancock* in preparation for launching on the Navy's first Alpha strike against communist facilities. Behind the 'Scooter' are two F-8Cs of VF-24, which formed part of the escort. Lr Cdr Greg Gregory is in NP 440 and Lt(jg) Tom Irwin is the pilot of NP 450, both F-8s carrying two AIM-9B Sidewinders

– sometimes four later on. One problem for the F-8Es in VF-211 was that if they returned with all four Sidewinders, their maximum landing weight dictated a max fuel load of 1200 lbs usually at, or below, "Bingo". So we sometimes ended up with the F-8Es flying lead, using their better air intercept radar, while we in the "Charlies" were the actual CAP. The "Charlies", without hardpoint wings, could come aboard with the four 'winders and 2500 lbs of fuel because of their lighter basic weight.

'The early strikes were fairly simple. The main group rendezvoused over the ship at various altitudes, and when everyone was aboard, off we went to the target at altitudes up to 24,000 ft.

'On one occasion, the A-1s had been launched early and were en route to the coast-in point for at least an hour before the jets launched. Due to stronger than forecast headwinds, they were still about 10 to 15 minutes from the target when the jets arrived overhead. We just continued orbiting the target at 20,000 ft until the "Spads" arrived and rolled in. There were no high-altitude air defenses at this point, except a few large-calibre guns which could only be used as flak barrage and were ineffective against high flying jets. The next year SAMs were introduced, and MiGs started coming out. The tactics changed and we came in at medium altitude – 3000-4500 ft – and went as fast as the slowest element of the strike group.'

The *Hancock*'s two F-8 fighter squadrons, VF-24 and VF-211, flew different models of the Crusader. VF-24 was equipped with the F-8C, which it used strictly in the traditional escort and CAP roles. VF-211 also used their F-8s as escorts, and, in fact, became the first US fighter squadron to encounter North Vietnamese MiGs, on 3 April 1965, when MiG-17s intercepted a bombing raid as related in the introduction. However, the 'Checkmates' of VF-211, who had obtained their 'Echoes' in February 1964, also used their fighters against ground targets too.

On 26 April two F-8Es from VF-211 escorted an RF-8A on a photo mission over Thanh Hoa. Lt (later Rear Adm) Rich Maughlin watched as the VFP-63 'photobird' began its run at very low altitude, perhaps to take forward fire pictures to show progress in bridge reconstruction following Air Force attacks – both services kept up cyclic raids on the bridge.

Following the photo run, the RF-8A pilot reported taking hits from 12.7 mm flak, which had taken off his outer wing panel. The two fighters fired their Zunis at the gun emplacement on the north embankment. Maughlin and his wingman, Dale Deweese, escorted the damaged RF-8A clear. Maughlin could see the gunner-director pointing to the jets rocketing over them at 500 knots, *below* ten feet. As they flew over the gun position Maughlin felt his jet shudder from a 37 mm strike on the vertical tail, which left a three-foot hole, barely missing vital hydraulic lines.

He joined on the RF-8A, and each pilot inspected the damage to the other's aircraft. The return to the ship was uneventful, and the three Crusaders recovered. However, the damage to Maughlin's F-8E (BuNo 150867) was so severe that his fighter's tail I-beam was bent *outside* the tail. The jet had to be catapulted off to the Philippines because the *Hancock*'s shipboard facilities could not repair such major damage.

The 'Black Knights' of VF-154, in *Coral Sea*'s Air Wing 15, were one of only two squadrons to fly the F-8D from carriers in Vietnam, the other being VF-111. VF-154 was also one of the first Navy Crusader squadrons, having received their F8U-1s (F-8As) in early 1957. It had participated in deployments to Formosa Strait in 1958 when a short war between Communist China and the Taiwanese government threatened peace in the area. On that occasion VF-154's F-8s flew from the *Hancock*, ready to take on the Communists should the efforts of the Taiwanese Air Force prove futile. However, direct US assistance was not needed.

During *Coral Sea*'s 1965 Vietnam cruise, VF-154 lost five Crusaders to enemy action, three of them in four days. Conversely, VF-211 had not lost any aircraft to the intense ground fire, and duly offered to help VF-154. It was the 'Checkmates'' assessment that the Black Knights were using peacetime delivery tactics – 80 per cent power, speedbrakes out, at 250 knots indicated air speed. VF-211 told VF-154 to make their runs as fast as possible, but the 'Black Knights' ignored the advice.

VF-154 (and VF-111) also participated in the *Flaming Dart* strikes of early February, raiding the North Vietnamese military barracks at Dong Hoi on the 11th – the facility was a major staging area for rebel infiltrators. Lt Cdr R W Shumaker's F-8D (BuNo 148633 NL 403) was hit by flak during the attack and he ejected and was captured, not returning until 1973.

Lt C E Wangeman was downed next in F-8D BuNo 148644 (NL 400) during a raid on a radar site on 26 March 1965, but he was recov-

A VF-111 F-8D fires Zuni rockets at Viet Cong positions in the South Vietnamese delta during a 1965 combat mission. The 'Sundowners' were the only F-8 squadron to use a sharkmouth around the prominent intake of the Crusader, the unit later applying the distinctive marking to their F-4Bs in 1972

ered after ejecting – Lt Cdr K E Hume was not so lucky three days later, being shot down and killed in F-8D 148668 (NL 408).

'Black Knight' CO Cdr William Donnelly was also knocked down by AAA on the same strike as Hume whilst flying F-8D BuNo 148642 (NL 407). He managed to go 'feet wet' before ejecting from his stricken fighter, spending a tense 45 hours in shark-infested waters before being rescued. Alone, in the dark, barely four miles off the enemy coast, Donnelly struggled to keep his life raft inflated and hide from patrolling North Vietnamese boats that were obviously searching for him. A Crusader pilot from the *Hancock* discovered Donnelly the following day, and an Air Force HU-16 Albatross flying boat launched from Da Nang to retrieve the water-logged skipper.

Lt Jack Terhune of VF-154 ejects from his crippled F-8D (BuNo 147899) after being hit on a raid on 11 October 1965 – Terhune was retrieved safely. The 'Black Knights' lost several aircraft during this cruise, including one flown by the unit CO, Cdr W N Donnelly, who was also rescued

Donnelly was just one of *three* squadron commanders from CVW-15 to be shot down during this cruise, VA-155's Cdr Jack Harris also ejecting from his A-4E (BuNo 150078) on the same 29 March strike and eventually being picked up by a submarine on plane-guard duty. Finally, Cdr Pete Mongilardi of VA-153, flying A-4C BuNo 149574 (NL 306), was killed in action when his Skyhawk was hit by AAA during an armed-reconnaissance mission on 25 June 1965.

The next VF-154 pilot lost over North Vietnam was Lt D A Kardell in F-8D BuNo 148673 (NL 413) on 9 May 1965, although his death remains officially recorded as 'cause unknown'. The final combat loss became the subject of perhaps the most familiar Crusader photo of the early war. Lt J A Terhune's F-8D BuNo 147899 (NL 406) had been hit by groundfire during a raid on 14 October, and although the jet remained airworthy long enough for its pilot to go 'feet wet', he could not recover back aboard *Coral Sea*. Watched by at least four other pilots from VF-154, Jack Terhune safely ejected from his stricken fighter and was swiftly plucked from the South China Sea – his ejection had been graphically photographed by his wingman.

This long cruise, totalling an incredible 331 days, was to be VF-154's only combat tour with the F-8. The squadron returned home and transitioned to F-4Bs in November.

Bonnie Dick moved up and down the Vietnamese coast from 'Dixie Station' to 'Yankee Station' and back again as requirements dictated. The carrier's combined det of RF-8As from the Navy's VFP-63 and the Marine Corps' VMCJ-1 was kept very busy, the first combat operations beginning on 26 May and continuing through to 2 July. Two weeks later the carrier was back on the line at 'Dixie Station' with two new F-8E squadrons. VF-191 and VF-194 used their F-8Es for both escort and ground attack roles, even though, to their frustration, parts for their jets and ground equipment were in short supply in depots in the Philippines – even the ship's LSO platform suffered from a lack of parts. Both units lost aircraft during this cruise, VF-191 having three F-8s downed by AAA and one by a SAM (plus a fifth jet destroyed in a fatal operational accident), whilst VF-194 lost three to flak and two in operational mishaps.

Oriskany made an eventful combat cruise from May to November 1965. She included three different Crusader squadrons in her Air Wing 16 – VFP-63's Det G and VF-162 were the two Navy squadrons, flying the RF-8A and F-8E respectively, whilst VMF(AW)-212, a Marine unit from Kaneohe Bay, Hawaii, also flew the F-8E, having converted from A-4s in 1963. *Oriskany*'s original second fighter squadron, VF-161, flew F-3 Demons, which were being rapidly replaced in the fleet by Phantom IIs. Thus, to keep a common aircraft in the wing for mission and maintenance considerations, the 'Lancers' were brought aboard in January 1965. The 27C carriers could not handle the bigger F-4s as well as the F-8.

Operating with a Marine squadron embarked was a unique situation for a Navy aircraft carrier. While Marine units had operated from carriers before – indeed, since the beginnings of US carrier aviation in the 1920s the Marines had 'gone to sea in ships', and had even had their own small carriers operating in the Pacific toward the end of World War 2 – the Navy had never consistently included Marines in the regular air-wing complement. Thus, the questions of keeping the Marine pilots carrier qualified and the very purpose of Marine aviation had to be continually addressed by Navy and Marine planners.

However, the 'Lancers', led by Lt Col Charles H Ludden, became an integral part of *Oriskany*'s air wing. In a unique turn of events, when Cdr

VF-194 CO, Cdr Bob Chew, is welcomed back after being shot down on 17 November 1965, *Bonnie Dick*'s skipper, Capt McClendon, being seen at far right. Chew ejected from his F-8E (BuNo 150308) after it was hit by groundfire at the Hai Duong Bridge during the delivery of Mk 84 2000-lb bombs. Also seen in this photo, from left to right, are; Dudley Moore, Ed Cichowitz, Charlie Schroeder, Buz Jewell, Ted Land and Rick Beslin

Aircraft of Air Wing 16 line the flightdeck of USS *Oriskany* (CVA-34) early in the war. Present are A-1Hs of VA-152, A-4Es of VA-164, F-8Es of VF-162 and VMF(AW)-212 and RF-8Gs of VFP-63. An A-4 is parked squarely on the centre-mounted bow elevator

Stockdale, commander of the wing, was shot down on 9 September 1965 in a VA-163 A-4E (BuNo 151134 AH 352), the most senior naval aviator in the wing was Lt Col Ludden. By prior agreement between Stockdale and Capt Bart Connolly, commanding officer of the *Oriskany*, Ludden, who was well liked and respected by his peers, would take over CVW-16 in such an event. Thus, Air Wing 16 had a Marine as its leader until 4 October, when Cdr Robert E Spruit assumed command.

VF-162 – THE 'HUNTERS' AT WAR

'Tuesday, May 25, 1965,

'Well, at long last, I can consider myself to be a combat pilot, as I made my first strike today. I didn't see anyone shooting at me, but I did blow up a house . . .'

Lt W F Flagg's letter to his wife described his premier mission in Vietnam, three weeks after *Oriskany*'s aircraft had fired their first shots in the 'O-Boat's' first combat cruise since the Korean War. He was a member of VF-162, and was the 'Hunters'' Quality Assurance (QA) officer in the squadron's maintenance department. He had remained in Japan in November 1963 when the carrier went to the South China Sea to cover any possibilities after the assassination of South Vietnamese President Diem.

Later, he found that getting parts for the F-8s was becoming a problem. However, the more the squadron flew its aircraft, the more the Crusaders remained operational. He decided that this 'up' status depended on the hydraulic seals. Typically, F-8s always leaked hydraulic fluid, but the leaks became more pronounced if the individual aircraft did not fly regularly. The seals would dry out and become brittle. Thus, when the jets did fly, the seals would crack and the fluid would run out.

Lt Col Charles Ludden was the senior aviator in CVW-16 when Cdr Stockdale was shot down. By prior agreement between Stockdale and the captain of the *Oriskany*, Ludden assumed the leadership of the air wing, and thus became the first Marine to command a carrier air wing since World War 2

During the initial stages of the 1965 combat deployment – which would last through to November, totally 256 days, with 210 days at sea – VF-162 pushed its fighter role because all the squadron pilots wanted a chance at a MiG. Their Marine counterparts in VMF(AW)-

212 assumed the role of the bombers, much to the amusement of the A-1 Skyraider pilots of VA-152. The A-1H 'drivers' claimed they dropped more bombs on the catapult than the F-8s did on their targets! Eventually, the 'Hunters' assumed more bombing duties.

Bud Flagg recalled, 'It was nice having a Marine squadron aboard. Like all Marine squadrons, they were very colourful. Initially, when they joined us, they had their share of excitement, but they completed the ORE and settled down to become one of the finest F-8 squadrons I ever had the pleasure of working with'.

Air-wing commander Jim Stockdale listened to the enthusiastic XO of the Marine squadron, Ed Rutty, who had flown with the Blue Angels, the Navy-Marine Corps flight demonstration team, in 1955.

'CAG', Rutty said, 'we are losing a plane a week trying to drop that Thanh Hoa Bridge with 500-lb bombs. They just bounce off the girders like little packages of brickbats. We can do better than that'. Stockdale waited as the Marine continued.

'I've been down in the ship's magazines, and the largest bombs down there are 2000-pounders. I've figured out a way to load them on Crusaders, as well as a way to arm and drop them.'

When Rutty asked Stockdale for permission to fly a mission with the huge Mk 84s, the Navy commander replied, 'I'll be right beside you on the cat and on the drop. Let me go talk to the captain'.

Although he led an air wing of half a dozen units, the CAG (a carryover from when the title was Commander Air Group) was responsible to the ship's captain. Thus, that august personage's permission and involvement was vital in all areas of operations, especially flight operations.

'Captain Bart Connolly', Stockdale remembered, 'was a real prince of a combat skipper. He said, "Go ahead and see if it works".'

With that, Stockdale let VMF(AW)-212 arm its F-8Es with 2000-lb bombs and plan an attack on the Thanh Hoa Bridge while he led a division of A-4 flak suppressors.

'I laughed as I saw those eight Crusaders waddling up the deck to take their cat shots.'

Unfortunately, the weather over the bridge was zero-zero, leaving Stockdale to redirect the attack toward alternate targets. The date was 9 September 1965, and over one of those alternate targets, Cdr Stockdale's A-4 was hit by groundfire, forcing him to eject into eight years of captivity and excruciating torture.

'I wondered how the fleet was doing with this arrangement of 2000-lb bombs under Crusaders. After my release I heard it was an unusual load, but it had served good purposes from time to time.'

Air Wing 5 returned to the Gulf of Tonkin in November 1965. Cdr Charles B McDaniel now led the 'Screaming Eagles' of VF-51. The unit participated in the Alpha strikes that were becoming almost daily routine – what some called the 'Doctor Pepper' era, with strikes at

An ordnanceman loads the cannons of an F-8E aboard *Oriskany*. The 20 mm guns were an effective strafing weapon, especially against lightly constructed barges, junks and trains

The deck crewman signals a successful trap as an F-8E of VMF(AW)-212 returns from a combat mission in 1965. This would be the last time a Marine squadron sailed in a carrier in combat until 1971

Air Wing 16 commander James Stockdale waits patiently in an F-8E of VMF(AW)-212 as ordnancemen check the Crusader's Zuni rockets

10, 2 and 4 – hauling bombs and rockets to targets in North Vietnam, including the Mk 84 2000-lb iron bombs.

On 22 December 1965, the air wing struck the Uong Bi thermal power plant north of Haiphong. Diving through intense flak, the strikers hit important areas of the main facility. The next day, *Tico* sent aircraft, including VF-51 and VF-53 F-8s, against the Hai Duong bridge, south of Hanoi. Along with other air wings, CVW-5 kept the pace up through to May 1966, when it returned to San Diego.

Although the F-8s had no bomb sight, they were found to be excellent flak suppressors, as well as ground-support aircraft, and the Crusader worked in these important roles throughout the war. Now-retired Rear Adm Flagg continues;

'We first hit "Yankee Station" in mid-May 1965. The action was really strong, although we only spent two days on "Yankee Station", and then went south to work in-country for two months. We later called it "Vacationland", because seldom did anyone shoot back at you. It was neat down there. We worked with a FAC. On occasion we were called on for flak suppression because we had our four 20 mm cannon.

'But one of my first engagements was with an Army company which had been pinned down by the Viet Cong. We came in over those guys – they had panels out – and I led the fighter sweep with all guns blazing. The report came back that we'd driven the communists off with our fire-power, and the Army was grateful. That was one of the few occasions I thought we'd done something other than shoot up the jungle.'

The F-8's four cannon were occasionally troublesome. Pilots started selecting the upper or lower pair of guns so that even if one set jammed, another pair was available. The jamming problem came largely from the effect of high-G on the ammunition belts. In high-G turns, the force made the linkage curl and bind, creating the possibility of a missed or jammed round. The big Zuni rockets also had problems. At the moment of ignition, they would shoot particles back toward the Crusader's tail and could cause damage.

On 7 October VMF(AW)-212 participated in an attack against the Vu Chua railroad bridge, between Hanoi and the Communist China border. Eight Marine F-8Es, each loaded with two 2000-lb bombs, made runs through intense anti-aircraft fire at the northern end of the structure, leaving the bridge and tracks twisted and mangled. Dropping 4000 lbs of bombs simultaneously caused problems at the moment of release, for the F-8 became momentarily unbalanced for a second or so, which created severe control problems, as well as overstressing the aircraft. However, a release mechanism was devised that allowed a one-two drop of the bombs.

Wearing his camouflage fatigues that substituted as flight suits for many naval aviators during the early combat cruises, air-wing commander James Stockdale checks his flight planning on 9 September 1965. A few hours later, whilst flying an A-4, he was shot down and captured (*Vice Adm James Stockdale, USN (Ret), via NMNA*)

The 'Lancers' flew their heavily-loaded Crusaders throughout November, toting Mk 84s whenever the targets required the huge bombs. On 5 November the Hai Duong rail-and-highway bridge received attention. Capt Harlan P Chapman in F-8E BuNo 150665 (WD 106) dropped his bombs only to be hit by groundfire that sent his Crusader tumbling out of control. He ejected and descended into a welcoming committee of civilians, who turned him over to the local militia. Chapman spent the next seven-and-a-half years as a PoW, having been promoted to lieutenant colonel during his imprisonment.

Capt Ross C Chaimson was hit by AAA 12 days later during a raid against the same bridge. although his F-8E, BuNo 150675 (WD 103), made it to the Gulf of Tonkin before its fuel ran out. The pilot tried stretching his glide through some clouds below, and incredibly, as he left the clouds behind, he spotted a carrier he thought was his own ship, the *Oriskany*, but it was the *Bon Homme Richard*. When he got as close as he dared, he punched out, one of *Bonnie Dick*'s helicopters picking him up.

Lt Col Ludden was strafing ground targets when small-arms fire shattered his canopy. At the time he was looking through his gunsight, head down. However, if he had been sitting erect, the shell would have decapitated him. As it was, fragments struck his eye and hip.

During a TARCAP mission in July, Flagg and his wingman spotted a glint of sunlight, which turned out to be one of the numerous small North Vietnamese trains. At the sound of the approaching American jets, the crew abandoned their train, the F-8s subsequently strafing the helpless target, walking their bullets up and down the length of the train. A flight of A-4s demanded that the F-8s depart and let them – the *real* bombers – drop their ordnance. Flagg told them they could have what was left of the train when he and his wingman was through. The HEI (high explosive incendiary) 20 mm had literally exploded the light box cars. The A-4s then laid down 500-lb bombs, straddling the helpless little engine and blowing it completely off the tracks and onto its side.

One young 'Hunter' pilot who was shot down not once but *twice* during his tour with VF-162. Lt(jg) Rick Adams, a native of Minneapolis, Minnesota, enjoyed his place as wingman for Cdr Dick Bellinger, the unit's XO who then became its CO. 'Belly One', as he was affectionately called, could be rough as a cob, but he and Adams seemed to mesh as a team. On 5 October 1965, Adams and the skipper were hunting SAMs . . . and they found them.

'Bulb', Bellinger called, 'get the hell out of here'. Referring to Adams' prematurely receding hairline, he was trying to warn his wingman of an on-coming missile that had just launched and seemed to be heading for Adams' F-8 (BuNo 150848 AH 227).

Lt(jg) Rick Adams returns from being rescued after being shot down on 5 October 1965. He is greeted by his squadronmates, including his skipper, Cdr Dick Bellinger, who hold replicas of the SA-2 SAM that got him. Lt Cdr Butch Verich holds a model of a gun – prophetic, because ten months later Adams would again be shot down, this time by communist groundfire, on 12 July 1966. Two days later, Cdr Bellinger would himself eject from his MiG-damaged F-8, whilst Lt Cdr Verich was also forced to eject from his crippled aircraft in August 1966 – the first of two combat ejections experienced by the latter pilot

Unfortunately, Adams' radio had gone out and he didn't hear Bellinger's call. He did see a flash as the missile flew past his aircraft just before exploding. Adams made a hard, right turn, pointing toward the South China Sea. He was lucky at least in one respect – if the SAM's 500-lb warhead had detonated any closer, it would have destroyed the F-8, giving him no chance to escape the blazing inferno that was now devouring the struggling fighter.

While Bellinger kept calling his number two, pleading with him to eject, Adams doggedly headed for the water. Like most American crews, he did not want to punch out over land, where he would probably be captured. The young pilot remembered having passed some destroyers on the way in, and now he hoped he could find them before ejecting.

Finally, the Crusader gave up the ghost and exploded. Adams ejected through the fireball, and he somersaulted through the air still attached to his seat. After a few seconds, the small drogue 'chute opened, then the larger, primary 'chute followed. Adams separated from his seat and began the descent toward the water. As he hit the sea, Adams released his harness and raft. Paddling over to his one-man raft, he looked up. 'Belly One' flew by waggling his wings in encouragement. He was so low that Adams could see into his skipper's cockpit!

The downed pilot hauled himself into the raft and began sorting out his situation, arranging his survival gear around him in the small, rubber, container. By now, Bellinger had alerted the rescue forces and was circling over Adams for the incoming helicopters. He was also worried about any enemy attempt to retrieve the downed aviator.

When a helo arrived, Adams rolled out of his raft into the water. However, he hadn't noticed how badly his hands were burned. Immersing them in the salt water made him cry out in surprised pain. The swimmer from the helicopter jumped in to help Adams get into the rescue sling,

In this September 1966 scene, enlisted ordnancemen wheel carts of bombs on *Oriskany*'s flightdeck. The weapons, which have yet to be fused, are of the retarded Snakeye variety, with tail fins that pop out after release. The VF-162 F-8Es in the background are probably tasked with escort and CAP duties in view of their full load-out of four Sidewinders

and before long the bedraggled aviator was on board the cruiser USS *Galveston* (CLG-3), where he received a preliminary examination and first aid for his burns.

Returning to *Oriskany* the next day, Adams was greeted by his squadronmates, who formed a gauntlet, complete with models of SAMs and flak guns. 'Belly One', meanwhile, smacked his wingman on the rear with a paper missile.

'How's it feel to be a hero, "Bulb"?' one of his friends asked. It was a facetious question, but Rick Adams was glad to be around to hear it.

Lt Boyd Repsher prepares for a flak suppression mission to the MiG field at Kep in 1966. Originally assigned to VF-11 to fly F-4s in the Atlantic Fleet, the young aviator got his orders changed and joined VF-194 as it left for Vietnam

Four months later, Rick Adams flew a mission that gained him the Distinguished Flying Cross. Again, he was dicing with SAMs, a battery of eight rocketing toward his flight, but he maintained his station through the intense defences. But the enemy was not through with him.

By July 1966, Adams was on his second tour with VF-162, one of only half a dozen members of the 1965 cruise to go on the second combat deployment. On 12 July he launched on a TARCAP mission in F-8E 150902 (AH 203), his target that day being near Haiphong, one of the most heavily defended areas in the north.

When his Crusader was apparently hit by small-arms fire, Adams faced another ejection. Fire spread from the tail to the forward fuselage as the F-8 rolled to the right.

'See you in a year', Adams called – he'd meant to say, 'ten years' – and he punched out at 2500 ft and 400 knots. As his Crusader plunged into a mountain, he landed near a village. Now, he was involved in a classic escape-and-evasion run for his life. The 'bad guys' were already looking for him, and he could hear them. He also knew that his friends had already called for the search-and-rescue (SAR) forces, and the helicopter was probably inbound. It was a question of who got to him first.

Four Skyraiders arrived escorting the H-3 helo, trying to keep the 'chopper' clear of enemy fire coming from all directions. The helo crew spotted Adams in the underbrush and sent the sling down for him. Strapping himself in, the F-8 pilot 'rode' the sling up through the trees, finally tumbling into the shuddering H-3 as more groundfire reached out.

As the two enlisted crewmen manned their machine guns, the battered, but thrilled Adams stared through a cabin window as the helo turned for home, escorted again by the protecting 'Spads', whose pilots fired their remaining ordnance at the gun positions on the ground.

Lt Bill Waechter, the H-3 co-pilot, was on his first mission into North Vietnam. 'Is it always this rough?', he asked Adams, unaware that this had been his passenger's *second* rescue in eight months.

'Seldom as rough as this', Adams replied, perhaps tongue-in-cheek.

Four hours after launching from *Oriskany*, a bedraggled Rick Adams was back on board, to be greeted once more by a line-up of squadron

HUD'N HUD'N in the Gulf of Tonkin in 1967 aboard *Tico*. VF-194's motto, displayed on the red banner, was more of a battle cry than a slogan. Front row, left to right; Joe Phaneuf, Dave Morris, Ed Cichowitz, Bill Conklin (CO), Bob Whitman (XO), Bob Cowles, William Reed, Dudley Moore. Rear row (left to right); Bob Springer, Jerry Houston, Jim Janes, Bob Hardee, Pete Brown, Boyd Repsher, Tom Wilburn, Jack Allen, Buz Jewell, Dick Nelson and Frank King

pilots. 'No one gets shot down twice', they hooted. They were wrong.

Rick Adams' second shootdown elicited a full-page article in *Time* magazine for 29 July 1966. Determined by the Navy to be 'combat limited', Adams was sent home. He flew with the Blue Angels in 1968 and eventually retired as a commander in 1982.

Lt Cdr Butch Verich was Rick Adams' flight leader on the July 1966 mission. He orbited his wingman as Adams flew a jet on fire from a combat zone for a second time. A month later, on 18 August 1966, Verich launched in F-8E 150300 (AH 211). Attacking river-barge traffic, Verich's jet was hit by small-arms fire. Twenty minutes after launching from *Oriskany*, the 40-year-old Verich ejected over the water.

In a strange twist of fate that would be repeated during the war, Verich's jet had downed a MiG-17 barely two months before when flown by VF-211's Phil Vampatella. The F-8E had been heavily damaged and Rick Adams had flown it to Japan to be repaired. Eventually transferred to VF-162, this was its first flight since its return to operational status.

Rescued, Verich kept flying. On 16 July 1967, in Crusader 150925, Verich attacked flak sites ahead of an A-4 strike. A SAM hit his F-8 and for the second time in less than a year, and like Rick Adams before him, Butch Verich made a combat ejection – his F-8 on this occasion was AH 201, the skipper's aeroplane. Again, like Rick Adams a year earlier, Verich was now on the ground in enemy territory, and they knew he was there. For 15 hours he hid from the enemy forces searching for him. After a night alone in the jungle, he was relieved to hear a force of F-8s, A-1s and A-4s swoop in and 'sanitise' the area around him.

'They tore the place up pretty well', he recalled. 'It was a little scary, but my friends were out there and I knew things would be OK.'

Verich fired a flare, alerting the H-3 crew from HS-2 off USS *Hornet* (CVS-12), who braved heavy fire to retrieve him after 20 minutes and three tries. Lt Neil Sparks, the helicopter commander, received the Navy Cross, and after two combat ejections, Butch Verich was sent home.

THE SAMS

Evidence of Soviet-built SA-2 surface-to-air missiles in North Vietnam was first revealed by an RF-8A from the *Coral Sea* on 5 April 1965. The site was 15 miles south-east of Hanoi, the North Vietnamese capital. However, permission to attack this new threat was refused, and it was not long before there was a profusion of SAM sites, their definitive six-pointed 'Star of David' layouts being easily discernible from the air.

Four months would pass before some form of action against the SAMs was allowed, and then, only after several aircraft had been lost, including two VA-23 A-4s from the *Midway*, which were recorded as the first official Navy losses to missiles.

VF-24's Lt(jg) Tom Irwin remembered early efforts to counter SAMs;

'As the SAM sites began to multiply, they became a big threat to the F-8s, as the early ECM (electronic countermeasures) equipment went first to the A-4s. I remember a jury-rigged set in 1966 which consisted of a D-cell battery-powered receiver with an antenna attached to the canopy with suction cups. You couldn't turn it on to test it until you were airborne because the ship's radar would burn it up on deck. The antenna came down around you like a spider's web during the catapult stroke.'

Most pilots felt they could avoid a SAM if they got a warning from an offshore ECM aircraft and they saw the missile. These warnings were in some kind of grid code from the ECM aircraft, usually EA-3s.

Retired-Capt Boyd Repsher flew 351 missions in South-East Asia as a member of VF-194 in 1966 and VF-211 in 1972. His 1966 cruise in USS *Ticonderoga* gave him an early introduction to the growing defences of the North Vietnamese, and the urgent need for effective countermeasures. Half of the Crusaders in Air Wing 19 had no ECM equipment, whilst those that did only had a launch-alert receiver that sounded a tone when lit by the SA-2's guidance radar. There was no directional information, so the pilot couldn't know where the threat was in relation to his aircraft.

During the cruise, F-8s were sent to Atsugi, Japan, where additional ECM modifications were made in Operation *Shoehorn*. Eventually, at least one jet in each section (usually two F-8s) had the updated ECM.

'I tried to get the flak suppression-TARCAP assignment whenever I could', Repsher recalled. 'Our ordnance was 20 mm, a pod of folding-fin rockets under each wing, two Zuni rockets and two Sidewinders on each fuselage mount. The Zuni was a *great* weapon you could put right down the enemy's throat.'

Dudley Moore had a close encounter with a SAM in 1966. It was one of those unusually clear days over Pak Six, not unlike south-

VF-194 F-8 'drivers' pose at Miramar before their 1967 cruise. Front row, from left to right; Dave Morris, Bob Cowles, Bob Chew (CO), Bill Conklin (XO), Ed Cichowitz and Frank Harrington. Rear row (left to right); Dick Nelson, Mike Newell, Pete Brown, Tom Wilburn, Boyd Repsher, G Gilbert, Jack Allen, Joe Phaneuf – Newell, Gilbert and Harrington were killed on this cruise

ern California. Then-Lt Repsher was the flight leader, and he and Moore crossed the coast south of Vinh on a MiG sweep. A MiG in those days was a rarity, but there was always hope. After some loose-deuce manoeuvring, the two F-8s were down to 'bingo' fuel, but they decided to make one more 180° turn before going 'feet wet'.

There was absolutely nothing going on, however, and they turned for home. Moore swung into a tactical wing position. Suddenly, he spotted a large squirt of dust on the ground with a large orange plume rising out of the middle of the cloud. SAM launch! Simultaneously, Moore hit 'burner, raised his wing 'droops' up, and keyed the mike.

'Sheepdog, SAM lifting off at nine o'clock. Get some speed on!' Repsher punched in his afterburner and pushed over in a 40° dive. The two F-8s were in a right bank, noses down, and accelerating. By now, Moore was at his lead's five o'clock, watching for the missile.

Both pilots had already seen SAMs in flight, but this was the first time they had had a ringside seat watching the full launch sequence. The SAM was at 3000 ft when the booster kicked off, and the tracking sequence began. There was no way of telling who it was locked on. Moore glanced at the mach meter – 600 knots. He said to Repsher, 'I'll call the turn'.

The missile was at terminal velocity, shooting a ten-foot flame, and coming fast. As it levelled nearly parallel to the ground, it became obvious that the SAM had locked on to Repsher.

'It's on you, "Rep". Break left, hard, now!' Everything seemed to slow down. The hardest part was waiting to time the hard roll so the missile couldn't match the turning angle.

Both Crusaders slammed on 6+ Gs as their noses went up and over, toward the vertical. The SAM was on them now. It was going to be close. As both F-8s rolled into the vertical 90°, the SAM pulled off Repsher and headed between the two Navy fighters. As the F-8s rolled into the missile, the SAM was right by Moore's canopy. He watched bug-eyed as it zipped across his windscreen, so close he could see big dents on it. As he stared at this beat-up missile, all he could think was, 'Bad QC(quality control)'!

The SAM flashed by as they rolled left, standing on left rudder. The Crusaders 'scooped out', and Moore watched the SAM out his right side. The missile, with nothing to guide on, tumbled crazily and headed straight up. It climbed about 1000 ft and exploded in a huge cloud of black smoke and flame against the brilliant sky.

Crusaders and Skyhawks formed a unique partnership against the SAMs, under the overall mission codename of *Iron Hand*. A-4s with AGM-45A Shrike missiles would lead their F-8 escorts in attacks against the sites. These attacks were extremely dangerous, for after the Navy's initial success with the beam-riding missiles, the Communists turned off their fire-control radars, thereby denying anything for the Shrikes to home on.

When the A-4s fired their Shrikes, the F-8s would follow the missiles right down toward the site, wait for missile impact, and then open up with their 5-inch Zunis and cannon, creating a devastating one-two punch. But many F-8s suffered major damage or loss during these SAM suppression runs. It was not a mission for the faint-hearted. The SA-2 was a 35-ft long missile with 350 lbs of high explosive in its warhead. Detonation within 200 ft of an aeroplane usually meant a kill.

MiG KILLERS

To a fighter pilot, the ultimate test and goal are one – engage another enemy fighter pilot and shoot him down. Once is sufficient to prove one's skill and mettle, whilst multiple kills are 'icing on the cake'. The war in South-East Asia was *not* a war of aerial engagements like portions of World War 2 and the Korean War. Indeed, no conflicts, with the possible exceptions of the Arab-Israeli War of 1973 and the Lebanon War of 1982, have approached these earlier struggles in the intensity of the respective wars in the air.

The air war in Vietnam saw two distinct periods of heightened activity – 1966-68, and the first six months of 1972. There were numerous reasons for these sporadic encounters between American and North Vietnamese fighters, but two in particular shaped the aerial engagements that were fought. Firstly, the sheer size of the VPAF militated against large encounters between opposing fighter forces, the North Vietnamese struggling in the first half of the war to have more than 20 to 30 interceptors available at any one time to use against the big strikes mounted by the US Navy and Air Force – by 1970, however, the VPAF's fighter force had grown considerably, numbering, according to varied sources, more than 250 MiGs of various models; MiG-17s, MiG-19s and MiG-21s. Secondly, US aerial assets in-theatre had to fight according to the self-imposed rules of engagement laid down by politicians in Washington

MiG killers from the Navy and Air Force line up for this photo at the end of *Bonnie Dick*'s highly successful, but costly, 1967 cruise. USAF Maj James A Hargrove was a member of a liaison staff, having previously downed a MiG-17 whilst flying an F-4C with the 366th TFW on 14 May 1967 – he had achieved his kill using an SUU-16 20 mm gun pod after firing Sidewinders and Sparrows at three other MiGs that were threatening a pair of F-105s. Lt Cdr Ted Swartz of VA-76 shot down a MiG-17 with Zunis from his A-4C – the only such kill of the war. The remaining F-8 MiG killers, from left to right, are; Paul Speer, M O Wright, Joe Shea, Bobby Lee and Phil Wood

which, like their earlier version in Korea, hamstrung and frustrated many American pilots who would have gladly pursued their adversaries across borders and over sensitive targets.

Here are examples of two Crusader pilots' experiences at different stages of the war that could have resulted in MiG kills but didn't. Lt Bud Flagg of VF-162 was on a BARCAP during the 1965 cruise;

'We all wanted a MiG so bad we could taste it. I was under the control of a destroyer, working south of Hong Ghe. The destroyer told us there was an aircraft coming from Kep, a major MiG base, and he vectored us to within five miles of the bogey, who turned north.

'We lit the 'burners and chased him, but at this time we weren't supposed to cross the 21st Parallel. Of course, in the air, you can't tell what parallel you're crossing, and I was in hot pursuit. We were gradually closing on him – I had him on radar. On the APQ-94 radar scope in the F-8, there was a little mark that told you when you were in range for a missile shot. The bogey was about 1-2 miles above that little mark and gradually coming down the scale. All I needed was another 5-10 minutes to close to get off a shot.

'But the destroyer controller yelled at me to break off because I was approaching the 21st Parallel. I pushed it until they really started screaming at me. I guess I actually did cross the parallel before turning around.'

After his tour with VF-211 in 1965, Jerry Unruh served with the 'Checkmates'' sister squadron, VF-24, in 1972. In both following episodes, the action began with radar contacts in the Americans' F-8Js and ended with a pair of frustrated fighter pilots;

'I was leading a flight of two when a MiG came out over the water. There was a safe zone in force where we couldn't go over land. We watched him until the controller said, "OK, he's still heading south. Take up an intercept, here we go . . ."

'We went after him – it was a MiG-17 – and he turned around and ran. He was quite a ways in front of us, but we had him on radar and locked him up. He ran for home and went "feet dry". We were still outside Sidewinder range, but close, really close. The controller told us we had crossed into the no-fly safe zone and to turn around.

'"Stand by", we said, but he was insistent. We just weren't closing fast enough, and he was still out of range. Within 30 seconds, Jehovah (the CTF commander's call sign) came up. "This is Jehovah. You are to turn around now!". We obediently turned back to the south and returned to the ship.

'During the debrief we learned that the MiG was just trying to sucker us into a MiG trap. Supposedly, there were several other MiGs ready to swing around behind us. We didn't know that at the time, although we thought they were just telling us that to make us feel better. But the intel guys said they were there.

'On another occasion, we were escorting the ELINT EC-121, an Air Force plane *Big Look*. He was doing maybe 180 knots over the Gulf, and he had worked himself much farther to the north than normal. We were circling over him, keeping him covered. We got calls for two red bandits – MiG-17s – coming out over the water by the North Vietnamese/China border. The EC-121 turned south, and I suggested we turn to engage the MiGs, but *Red Crown* said no, that our job was to escort the '121.

'We worked our way south, with the MiGs slowly closing behind us. After the '121 was fairly well south, I said to the controller, "Hey, we're pretty far south now, how about letting us take them on?"

'"OK, you can do it."

'We turned around, and so did the bogies. We picked up the MiGs on radar at about ten miles. We closed to about seven miles, then five miles. It was going well. Any time we'd be in range for a Sidewinder shot, although I couldn't see the MiGs. At that point, our controller told us there were two MiG-21s airborne from a PRC base on Hainan Island, heading for the '121. We immediately broke off the chase to protect the USAF plane. As we closed, they turned away back to Hainan.'

The F-8 fighter could claim to be the last gun-armed, air-superiority single-seat fighter in naval service. Albeit highly successful, the F-4 Phantom II carried an all-missile armament as a result of a decision in the 1950s to do away with guns in favour of the more sophisticated air-to-air missile. Originally a single-seater, the Phantom II added another crew member – the radar intercept officer (RIO) – to operate its radar system. Ultimately, the RIO's main contribution to the Phantom II concept proved to be simply another pair of *human* eyes to help the pilot during aerial engagements. It was not until the development of the Grumman F-14 Tomcat that the pilot truly needed a dedicated, specially-trained, crewman behind him to operate the weapons radar, and to successfully fly the fleet-defense mission.

A friendly, but intense, rivalry developed between F-4 and F-8 crews. When VF-51 began transitioning from Crusaders to rather dilapidated and war-weary F-4Bs in 1971, several F-8 alumni in the squadron couldn't hide their lack of enthusiasm for the two-seater. Cdr Tom Tucker, himself a former RF-8 driver, and the subject of one of the most well-photographed combat rescues on record when he was shot down over Haiphong in 1966, led the change.

While Navy Phantom IIs accounted for 36 MiGs and two An-2 Colt transports, and the Marines got one MiG in a Marine F-4, the F-8 was officially credited with 18 confirmed MiG kills, as well as an occasionally loosely credited kill in 1972. This last incident involved a MiG-17 pilot bailing out of his fighter as two F-8s approached.

It is interesting to note that all the Crusader's official kills came within a relatively short two-year period, for after the last score on 19 September 1968, all Navy MiG kills were by Phantom IIs (except for six kills by Talos and Terrier shipboard SAMs in 1972 against an abortive series of attacks by a special unit of MiG-17 pilots). The main reason for this lack of additional Crusader kills, as any Crusader alumnus will confirm, was the lack of 'vectors' for the frustrated F-8 pilots, who spent the last three years of the war flying from the smaller carriers. Largely relegated to flying ground-attack sorties, with occasional bomber-escort flights, F-8 pilots invariably had to stay with the bombers even when MiGs appeared in their area.

The powerful Phantom II could carry more bombs, besides its regular load of Sidewinder and Sparrow missiles, than the F-8, and had assumed its intended place as the fleet's main fighter as the war ground on. Thus, the F-8 pilots, though primed and ready to engage the North Vietnamese MiGs, found themselves crying for a chance to go after the MiGs. But, in

Cdr Hal Marr returns from his MiG-killing mission in NP 103, his highly decorated white helmet sporting red checks, in keeping with VF-211's nickname, 'Checkmates'

their time, the F-8 'drivers' were the leading destroyers of communist aerial hardware.

Indeed, in his fine book, *Clashes: Air Clashes Over North Vietnam, 1965-1972* (Naval Institute Press, 1997), former USAF F-4 pilot, and veteran of more than 300 missions in Vietnam, Marshall L Michel III declared, that considering '. . . the F-8 pilots' kills per engagement (the highest of any fighter in the war) and their high percentage of in-the-envelope missile firings, it is not difficult to conclude that the F-8 pilots were the best air-to-air pilots in the theater during *Rolling Thunder*'.

The Crusader opened its score-sheet on 12 June 1966 when Cdr Harold L Marr, commanding officer of VF-211, shot down a MiG-17 while flying escort for an A-4 strike. Watching the Skyhawks of VA-212 and VA-216 make their runs, Marr, his wingman, Lt(jg) Phil Vampatella, and another two-aircraft section of F-8s from VF-24, led by Lt Cdr Fred Richardson (one of the Navy's few black aviators at the time), held at 1500 ft under clouds. As the bombers came off their target and rejoined their escorts, Vampatella called out approaching MiGs from behind, at the seven o'clock position. The four MiGs were at about 2000 ft. Cdr Marr described the fight;

'We pull hard into them and the fight's on. Two MiGs split off, and we pass the other two head on. I fire a short burst of cannon at one MiG, more for courage than anything else – just to hear my four cannons bang.

'We're doing about 450 knots and pulling seven to eight Gs and reverse hard right in a sharp scissors. I get a good 90° deflection gun shot, but my cannon misses again, and Phil goes after one and I after the other.

'Now I'm at 2500 ft at his eight o'clock and the MiG is down around 1500 ft with nowhere to go. I fire the first of my two Sidewinders, but the missile can't hack it and falls to the ground.

'The MiG has been in 'burner for four or five minutes now and is mighty low on fuel, so he rolls and heads straight for his base. I roll in behind, stuff it in 'burner, and close at 500 knots. At a half-mile, I fire my last 'Winder, and it chops off his tail and starboard wing. He goes tumbling end over end. The poor pilot doesn't have a chance to eject.'

The two MiGs that Marr and Vampatella engaged were clean externally, carrying no wing tanks or missiles. One MiG was all silver, the other grey – both MiG-17s carried red stars on their upper wingtips, and yellow fuselage markings aft of the wings.

Marr aimed his initial cannonfire – approximately 150 rounds – at the silver MiG, which appeared to be the element leader. Marr's first AIM-9D Sidewinder may have homed in on a cloud's reflection before falling off to the right. He actually fired his second Sidewinder at 4500 ft, half a mile behind the MiG, which crashed at the edge of a small town on the bank of a river.

The second MiG had been the target of VF-24's Lt Cdr Fred Richardson, who had fired both Sidewinders but missed. His wingman, Lt(jg) Denis C Duffy Jr, also fired a Sidewinder at the twisting grey MiG, but although this missile seemed to guide properly, it failed to reach the target before falling off.

Having destroyed the MiG leader, Cdr Marr saw two other MiG-17s orbiting above him at nine o'clock, one grey and the other in the green-brown camouflage occasionally seen during the war. He climbed to 6000 ft and engaged this second pair of MiGs, firing 25-30 cannon rounds. He saw fragments coming off the right wing of one of the MiGs, but he quickly ran out of ammunition and had to break off, claiming only a probable.

There has always been some uncertainty about Cdr Marr's 'probable' second kill. Although the score was apparently *confirmed* soon afterward, it was never officially credited because of sensitive sources. However, after more than 30 years what could it matter now? It would seem that Hal Marr does have two confirmed MiG kills, and if that is the case, the long-held number of 18 'official' kills for the Crusader is off by one, and by two if you count the 'bail-out' kill of May 1972. Thus, the F-8's score is at least 19 and maybe 20 – for more on this subject see chapter six.

An ecstatic Marr claimed the traditional victory fly-by when he returned to the *Hancock*, along with his wingman, Lt(jg) Vampatella. The F-8 had gained its first kill. In his excitement, Marr had forgotten to drop his tailhook, normally a five-dollar fine, and had to make a second approach. Capt Jim Donaldson, *Hancock*'s CO, sportingly offered to pay the fine.

CHANCY'S AND VAMPATELLA'S KILLS

One of the most colourful Crusader-MiG engagements of the entire war occurred just nine days after Cdr Marr had downed the F-8's first kill(s), and involved his wingman on the 12 June fight, Phil Vampatella. On 21 June, 11 *Hancock* aircraft flew a strike into North Vietnam. The raiders were divided into two groups – a two-jet flight (an RF-8A and its VF-211 F-8E escort), which would make a reconnaissance run of the railway north-east of Hanoi, and six A-4s with three VF-211 F-8E escorts.

The three 'Checkmate' Crusader strike-escort pilots were Lt Cdr Cole Black, Lt Gene Chancy and Lt(jg) Vampatella. As the A-4s ran in toward their target, word came that the RF-8A (BuNo 146830 PP 909) flown by Lt L C Eastman had been shot down. After making sure that the A-4s were clear of their target, the three F-8 pilots hastened to the site of the RF-8A's crash, taking radio cuts on the escort F-8E's radio transmissions. Lt Cdr Black and Lt Chancy orbited over the site, while Lt(jg) Vampatella took the wingman position for the photo escort, whose pilot, Lt Dick Smith, had assumed the role of SAR (Search and Rescue) commander. The four VF-211 F-8s remained at 1500 to 2000 ft above the crash site.

The situation became complicated as the A-4s began calling out SAM launches and MiG warnings. The F-8s also began drawing flak – 37 mm, 57 mm and probably 85 mm fire. Vampatella felt his plane shudder as he took a hit, but he remained on station for 10-12 minutes.

Smith and Vampatella saw the downed photo-pilot's 'chute, and Black and Chancy climbed to gain better radio communication with the

Lt(jg) Phil Vampatella (centre) listens to a brief in the VF-211 ready room before a mission in June 1966. Note the large squadron patch on his right shoulder. Lt Bobby Hulse is in the row behind, wearing a green nylon flight jacket, while 'nugget' pilot, Ens Ray Lorang, is on Vampatella's left. Hulse was Lt Unruh's wingman during the MiG engagement on 3 April 1965

incoming SAR helicopter. Reaching 6000 ft, Chancy heard a SAM warning, and he and his leader remained at that altitude. Black asked about the F-8s' fuel state and ordered Smith and Vampatella to find a tanker. This left Black and Chancy (in F-8E 150910) orbiting at 2000 ft above the downed RF-8. They spotted an orange signal flare, presumably set off by the photo pilot, about half a mile from the crash site.

Then, Lt Cdr Black saw two MiG-17s (probably from the 923rd Fighter Wing, based at Kep) sliding in from the south, out of the clouds at the F-8s' two o'clock. The North Vietnamese fighters were very close, perhaps half a mile, and 500 ft above the Crusaders. Black levelled his wings and began firing his cannon, but the MiGs passed close to Chancy, their guns blazing. Chancy quickly fired his own guns as he crossed over his leader, left to right. The MiGs had apparently waited until the Crusaders had left their high-altitude station during the A-4 attack, and were in orbit, at low fuel state, above the RF-8 on the ground. The F-8s would be at a disadvantage at such a low height, and also dangerously low on fuel.

Lt Chancy's desperate fire hit the MiG wingman as the section slashed through the Crusaders, blowing a wing off the MiG.

'He was so close', Chancy later recalled, 'I could have counted his teeth. It was a very effective attack'. Chancy also got a harsh tone and fired one Sidewinder, but the missile failed to guide.

It would be a while before Gene Chancy's score would be changed from a probable to a confirmed kill, since the MiG was not actually seen to crash, and other participants in the fight were to busy or too distant to observe the action. However, Capt Donaldson told him to go to Saigon for the traditional press conference that followed every American MiG score. Many months later, a Vought rep called Chancy to tell him he owed the lieutenant the special Vought pin the company gave to Crusader MiG killers. The lapel pin consisted of an F-8 silhouette with a red ruby.

Vampatella's Crusader was badly damaged by flak *before* he turned back toward the MiGs. Note the large chunk out of the starboard stabilator and the pock marks from shell shrapnel. After being repaired in Japan and re-assigned to VF-162, BuNo 150300 was again hit by enemy fire on 16 July 1967 and its pilot, Lt Cdr Butch Verich, forced to eject. Vampatella's MiG-killer became one of several victors that were ultimately 'bagged'

Although Gene Chancy's kill has always been listed as a missile score, he is certain he downed the MiG by his initial gunfire, especially since his single Sidewinder did not guide properly. This would make him one of only two Crusader 'drivers' who could claim a guns kill over Vietnam.

Unfortunately, Chancy's elation at his success quickly evaporated for he could not find his leader. Lt Cdr Black's F-8E (BuNo 149152 NP 100) had been hit by the lead MiG, and he had ejected. To Chancy's dismay, the SAR helo, originally sent to recover the RF-8 pilot, got lost and never showed up. Both Black and the RF-8 pilot, Lt Eastman, were captured and remained PoWs until 1973. Chancy had to leave his leader on the ground and return to the ship.

Lt Gene Chancy sits in his F-8E. Although he scored the third ***official*** MiG kill of the war, confirmation and credit were a long time coming

'Those guys are what Americans are made of', he said, recalling the trials of all the PoWs.

Despite suffering the loss of his formation leader, Gene Chancy had evened his score with the Communists, for nearly eight weeks earlier he had ejected from his damaged F-8E (BuNo 149169 NP 100) after taking hits from an enemy flak site protecting a radar facility on an island he and his flight leader were preparing to strafe. His fighter's utility hydraulics were gone and there were cockpit warning lights everywhere. He punched out as the Crusader snap-rolled inverted.

Chancy descended by parachute into the water and was rescued by a helicopter, whose crew said they had taken fire from the same island site. This was Chancy's second ejection, for in December 1963 he had bailed out of a VF-124 F-8C (BuNo 145577) near El Centro, in desert California, after losing several vital electric and hydraulic systems.

Returning to the MiG engagement in June 1966, the fight had not ended with Chancy's kill. Hearing Lt Cdr Black's call of 'MiGs!', Smith and Vampatella had hauled their jets around and returned to the mêlée, even though Vampatella's F-8 (BuNo 150300) was damaged. Nearing the action, they saw a section of two MiGs at 2000 ft in a diving right turn. Smith called a warning.

'F-8, you have a MiG on your tail!' He could see the MiG's guns firing, followed by the F-8 bursting into flames. It was Cole Black going down.

A second MiG section now appeared, and Lt Smith tried to engage the leader, but his guns failed while in a high-G turn. Vampatella, meanwhile, had looked back to find another MiG saddled in on his tail, in gun range, and firing. Vampatella tried to scissor with the MiG but had to limit his turns to five Gs because of the previous battle damage.

The MiG stayed with the F-8, and although low on fuel, Vampatella lit his afterburner, disengaged the MiG, and headed east at 600 knots. Safe for the moment, he found the Crusader getting harder to fly, however. The MiG was more than a mile behind, and the North Vietnamese pilot seemed to have turned back toward home, probably low on fuel himself.

Seizing the opportunity, Vampatella reduced his speed and turned back toward the departing MiG. At approximately three-quarters of a mile, He tried one Sidewinder, then the second. The second finally came off the rail and guided straight toward the MiG, detonating immediately behind the enemy fighter, which crashed.

After hitting the tanker with only 300 lbs of fuel remaining, Lt Chancy escorted Vampatella back to the *Hancock* 60 miles away. Vampatella tried to refuel, but the tanker could give him only a bare minimum. It was uncertain if he could get back. However, he landed safely, and post-flight inspection revealed that his jet had been hit in the vertical tail by 37 mm fire, with about 80 small holes dotting the F-8's rear surfaces.Phil Vampatella received the Navy Cross for his courage and skill, the second award of the Navy's highest decoration for Vietnam aerial action – the first Navy Cross for aerial combat in Vietnam had been awarded to A-6 bombardier Lt(jg) Brian Westin of VA-85 for action on 27 April 1966. The Medal of Honor – the highest *American* award for valour – is given in the name of the US Congress. Both Vampatella's and Chancy's F-8s were eventually lost to enemy flak in 1966 and 1967 respectively.

Although these three June 1966 engagements decisively opened the Crusader's score card, the problems encountered with the F-8's armament – especially the troublesome cannon – brought an in-depth analysis of the combats by the Commander-in-Chief, US Pacific Fleet.

The study indicated there had been 11 attempts to fire Sidewinders in the two fights, but two missiles had failed completely and one had a delayed firing. Three attempts to fire the 20 mm cannon resulted in failure, one complete, and two stoppages after only a few rounds. Only Cdr Marr was able to successfully expend all his ammunition. The report concluded

'. . . 13 of the 24 guns experienced some failure. Two of the six aircraft experienced a malfunction on the first round. One pilot voluntarily ceased fire after firing one fourth of his ammunition, and only one pilot was able to expend all his rounds.

'20 mm guns in F-8 aircraft have generally been regarded as a weapon secondary to Sidewinder for air-to-air engagements. The results of this study . . . show the opportunities for F-8 aircraft to fire 20 mm in engagements typical in South-East Asia may approach the opportunities for them to fire Sidewinder.'

That final observation proved unfounded. While the Air Force experienced many successes with 20 mm cannon, particularly with the F-105, which included an integral gun in its original design, the Navy's kills were, with the exception of perhaps two or three F-8 kills, all scored with missiles, predominantly Sidewinders, which came to be fairly dependable weapons. The other main missile, the AIM-7 Sparrow, which the F-8s didn't carry, was used only by F-4s. While supposedly more sophisticated – and ultimately more expensive – the Sparrow enjoyed little success, and subsequently low confidence from the Navy's fighter crews.

F-8 MiG killer Robert Kirkwood commented, 'One of the ironies of the F-8's story was that it was called, "the last of the gunfighters". But it was equipped with an unreliable, inaccurate, ineffective gun system'. Also ironic was that Kirkwood was the only Crusader pilot officially credited with a guns kill!

VF-111 on board *Oriskany* in 1966. Front row , from left to right; Pete Peters, unknown, Lloyd Hyde, Bob Rasmussen (XO), Dick Cook (CO), unknown, Bob Grammer, Bill McWilliams and Norm Levy. Rear row, left to right; Frank Mosoc, Dick Schaffert, Andy Anderson, Ed van Orden, Ramsey Rims, Wil Abbott, John Sands, Cody Ballasteria, 'Tooter' Teague, Bob Pearl and Jay Meadows. Lt(jg) van Orden was killed in action, while Capt Abbott was an Air Force exchange officer who was shot down by MiGs and interned. Lt Hyde, Lt(jg) McWilliams, Lt Cdr Levy and Lt(jg) Ballasteria died in the fire of 26 October 1966

Cole Black's loss was one of only three *confirmed* F-8 losses to MiGs during the entire war. Later, on 14 July 1966, a VF-162 F-8E (BuNo 150908 AH 202) flown by squadron CO Cdr Dick Bellinger, and on 5 September, a VF-111 F-8E (BuNo 150896 AH 106), were shot down by MiGs, Air Force Capt W K Abbott, on exchange duty, becoming a PoW after the latter action. It is of interest to report that no RF-8s were lost to North Vietnamese fighters, all 20 VFP-63 combat losses resulting from flak and SAMs.

BELLINGER GETS A MIG

As briefly detailed above, the VF-162 loss to MiGs involved the squadron's colourful skipper, Cdr Dick Bellinger. At 42, Bellinger was a little older than the average fighter skipper, but then he had flown in World War 2 as an Army Air Force bomber pilot, transferred to the Navy after the war, and flown combat in Korea. Now in his third war, Bellinger knew this was probably his last chance to achieve an aerial kill.

The July shootdown had come after a high-speed chase over downtown Hanoi, with one 'Hunter' pilot dragging a MiG that had locked onto his tail. Lt Cdr Chuck Tinker only succeeded in evading his pursuer by dodging buildings at 50 ft above the densely populated city. Tinker did not have a working radio – the flight had known this before going over the coast – and when he saw yet another MiG on his CO's tail, he could not warn him.

The MiG peppered the commander's Crusader, Bellinger ducking into a cloud and limping away, trying to make Da Nang before his fuel ran out. He was unable to refuel from an orbiting tanker because of the dam-

Cdr Dick Bellinger exuberantly describes his MiG-21 kill to Lt Dick Wyman as they walk away from the former's Crusader, followed by other squadron members. Bellinger was a colourful pilot and squadron commander in the same realm as the Marine Corps' 'Pappy' Boyington

age to his aircraft, and he ejected from his crippled Crusader 40 miles from the mainland.

On 9 October Bellinger (flying F-8E 149159 AH 210) led three other 'Hunter' Crusaders acting as escort for an A-4 strike from the carrier USS *Intrepid* (CVS-11). An E-1B Tracer vectored the escorts toward incoming MiGs, which turned out to be MiG-21s, which were only just entering service with the VPAF, and represented a considerable jump in technology for the beleaguered communist air service.

One of the delta-winged MiGs split-essed toward the ground, and Bellinger followed, firing two Sidewinders. He was at a dangerously low altitude and could not watch the progress of his missiles as he zoomed over the steaming jungles. But one of the Sidewinders found its mark, and the MiG-21 crashed into the rice paddies below, marking the first Navy kill over the advanced MiG. Dick Bellinger flew back to the *Oriskany* to a tumultuous welcome from his ship and squadron. One week later, Secretary of Defense Robert McNamara, on a Vietnam tour, came aboard to personally award Bellinger the customary Silver Star for his MiG kill.

Bellinger had many sides to him, and had as many supporters as detractors – there was very little room for shadings. To many people in his squadron, Bellinger could be a raging, sometimes out-of-control, bull, but to many others, his name evokes fond memories.

Serving under Bellinger on this cruise was Bud Flagg, who recalls that 'Bellinger *was* a colourful character. But he flew the F-8 well and commanded the squadron well. He was always there to do the job. . . He was tops'.

Mrs Dee Flagg, who, like so many of the young wives of the period, lived through her husband's combat deployments with a mixture of fear, courage and ultimate hope, remembers Dick Bellinger and his wife, Norma, as 'great people'.

'He was really a Santa Claus', she recalls, 'although he obviously had a different face when leading the "Hunters".'

F-8s did not score again until May 1967, by which time, the American bombing offensive against the North Vietnamese was in full swing. Daily strikes seemed to be hurting the North's ability to continue the war, even with major restrictions levied by Washington as to what type of targets could be hit, and where and when. Disregarding the high loss rate, and the uncertain fate of US crews after they bailed out of their stricken machines, the Americans hurled themselves at their objectives.

May 1967 was an especially intense period, and all squadrons from every ship on the line participated in a number of large raids. The MiGs were active, and the engagements were sharp and intense. It seemed that whatever trepidations the pilots in the VPAF MiG-17s and MiG-21s might have had at first had now been supplanted by experience and deter-

NP 110, 'Mo' Wright's MiG killer, taxies up to the catapult

mination borne of two years of dogfighting with their American opponents.

The *Bon Homme Richard*'s Air Wing 21 was in the forefront of Navy successes, beginning on 1 May – the traditional Communist holiday. Lt Cdr M O 'Mo' Wright of VF-211 shot down one of three MiG-17s 'bagged' on this day while he was escorting *Iron Hand* A-4s 35 miles north of Hanoi in F-8E BuNo 150923 (NP 104). He got on the MiG's tail as it attacked an A-4 and fired a Sidewinder, which sent the jet tumbling into the ground. Air Force Capt Ron Lord, serving an exchange tour with the 'Checkmates', flew with Wright.

'It was a beautiful hit', Lord said later. 'The MiG just came apart at the seams'. Later, Lord himself chased a MiG off another A-4 with his cannon. Lt Cdr Wright's Crusader was another MiG-killer that the enemy eventually nailed when, as an F-8J (NP 102), it was shot down by flak on 20 June 1972 over South Vietnam. VF-211 CO Cdr Jim Davis ejected and was rescued.

Besides Wright's kill, Lt Cdr T R Swartz got his A-4C (BuNo 148609 NP 685) behind a MiG, the VA-76 pilot firing three separate Zunis – normally ground-attack weapons – at the MiG, which dived into the ground. Ted Swartz was actually a Crusader alumnus, with 2000 hours in the F-8. He had been an instructor and LSO (landing signal officer) for VF-174, the east-coast F-8 training squadron. While at Cecil Field, Swartz instructed many of the Crusader pilots who ultimately fought in Vietnam.

When his tour was about to end, however, Swartz was convinced the Vietnam War would be an attack

USAF exchange pilot Capt Ron Lord (left) and Lt Cdr 'Mo' Wright go over their MiG encounter. Their sweaty flight suits attest to the intensity of the day's work

Cdr Paul Speer confers with a deck crewman after returning from a mission in on 4 May 1967

pilot's war, and he asked to be sent to an A-4 squadron. But, he remained a fighter pilot, and when the opportunity came, he took it, becoming the only A-4 pilot to score a MiG kill in Vietnam.

The F-8's best days came next – 19 May 19 and 21 July – when seven pilots shot down seven MiGs, accounting for nearly half of the entire Crusader tally during the war.

It had been a hard cruise – CVW-21 had lost 23 aircraft and 18 pilots. The mission for 19 May involved A-4/F-8 *Iron Hand* strikes against heavy concentrations of SAM and flak positions (37 mm, 57 mm and 85 mm), complicated by substantial MiG opposition. Six Crusaders – three apiece from VF-211 and VF-24 – provided the escort, and one F-8E from VF-211 (BuNo 150930 NP 109) was brought down by a SAM, its pilot, Lt Cdr Kay Russell, being captured. The five remaining F-8s sustained damage from flak and MiG cannonfire during the mission.

In the air-to-air engagements, the two *Bonnie Dick* squadrons scored two MiG-17s apiece. VF-24's Lt Cdr (later Rear Adm) Bobby Lee and Lt Cdr (later Capt) Phillip Wood in F-8Cs BuNos 146981 and 147029 (NP 405) respectively, VF-211's skipper, Cdr (later Rear Adm) Paul Speer (F-8E BuNo 150348 NP 101) and Lt(jg) Joseph Shea (F-8E BuNo 150661) each fired Sidewinders.

As the two A-4s from VA-212 (squadron CO Commander Homer Smith and Lieutenant(jg) Steve Briggs) delivered their Walleyes against the SAM sites, Cdr Speer spotted a MiG and turned into him. In full afterburner, the VF-211 skipper engaged the North Vietnamese fighter in a series of manoeuvres until the MiG pilot finally offered the Crusader pilot a shot. Speer's first Sidewinder fell away, but his second missile hit the MiG in the tail. The jet soon began streaming fire, then rolled over and crashed into the ground.

Cdr Speer talks with his wingman, Lt(jg) Joe Shea, about their two MiG kills on 19 May 1967

Joe Shea, in the meantime, had spotted another enemy fighter, warning, 'There's a MiG among us. Nobody get excited'. Cdr Speer gave his wingman the lead, and the 'jaygee' also fired two Sidewinders, both of which hit the MiG, sending it also into the Hanoi suburbs. This series of engagements by VF-211 and VF-24 ran the length of the Hanoi-Haiphong complex, occasionally at very low altitude.

Lee's and Wood's kills were the first for their squadron. Lee was Wood's flight leader as they escorted A-4s on a strike against Hanoi. Nearing the target, they spotted a MiG-17 closing on an A-6 from the *Kitty Hawk*, which was also on the raid. In a tight turn, Lieutenant Wood fired a Sidewinder, but the missile fell off harmlessly because of the Gs. The MiG pilot dove for safety. Another MiG-17 came in behind Wood and began firing. He hauled his F-8 around and fired another AIM-9D. This missile hit the MiG, sending it diving toward the ground. The enemy pilot ejected, but his 'chute streamed.

Unable to get back to his carrier, shot up and low on fuel, Lt Wood took interval in the *Kitty Hawk*'s landing pattern and trapped on the big-deck carrier. He was warmly greeted by the crew of the A-6, whose tail he had cleared of the first MiG – Wood returned to *Kitty Hawk* as her CO in 1985. His F-8 was a strike, however. There were bullet holes behind the cockpit, the engine and avionics were 'trashed', and the Navy decided it was not worth repairing the fighter, which was taken below to the hangar bay to be off-loaded at Cubi and scrapped. Wood took advantage of a helo ride back to his own carrier, where the festivities were already in progress over the latest MiG kills.

Phil Wood preflights one of his Crusader's Sidewinders. He carried only three missiles on his MiG engagement because the Sidewinder on the upper left rail didn't pass its pre-flight checks and was never loaded. The first missile Wood fired was in the same position shown here – the lower left rail

Lt Cdr Bobby Lee and his wingman, Lt(jg) Kit Smith, had gone after what Lee called 'the biggest flak site I had ever seen'. At 3000 ft, they fired their Zunis, hitting the SAM's radar vans. As the two F-8 pilots pulled out of their runs at 700 ft, a MiG-17 crossed their noses. Lee fired a Sidewinder, which cut the MiG in half. 'The entire tail section rotated to the outside of his turn, and I knew he was dead', Lee said later. When he returned to the *Bonnie Dick*, Lee's ordnancemen who had loaded the Sidewinder onto his F-8 gave him the AIM-9's umbilical cord as a souvenir.

Two months later on 21 July, four Air Wing 21 pilots scored. While proceeding to their target – a POL storage facility at Ta Xa north-west of Haiphong – CVW-21 A-4s were attacked by an estimated force of ten MiG-17s. The combined VF-24 and VF-211 escort waded into the interceptors. VF-24's newly-arrived executive officer, Cdr Marion H Isaacks, got above and behind one MiG. He tried twice to fire his Sidewinders – he was carrying a full load of four – but the first AIM-9 failed to guide, and the second malfunctioned and didn't fire. Frustrated, he tried once

Phil Wood's MiG-killer F-8C aboard *Kitty Hawk*, so badly damaged that it was struck from service. The photo was taken by the pilot (Sam Sayers) of the A-6 that Lt Wood rescued from the attentions of a MiG-17. Sayers autographed the photo with the message, 'A grateful A-6 pilot owes you a drink'

'Red' Isaacks poses in an F-8 after his MiG kill – note the temporary name card

more. The third missile came off the rail and tracked perfectly, right up the MiG's tailpipe. The enemy fighter went down in a fireball.

Staring at the fireball, Isaacks nearly became someone's kill, himself, when one of the MiG's wingmen drove in, firing all the way. Isaacks kicked right rudder, turning to meet his attacker. With his windscreen full of MiG intake, the VF-24 XO gaped as the North Vietnamese pilot turned away at the last moment and snap-rolled for the deck, leaving Isaacks with a badly damaged Crusader (F-8C BuNo 147018 NP 442).

His jet had a small fire near the right aileron, fed by hydraulic fluid. However, the blaze remained confined to the small area on the wing, and after the fluid had been burned it extinguished itself as Isaacks flew back to the carrier. He summed up the air war during a visit to Vought made soon after his MiG kill.

'The MiGs are good for morale, I guess. There's more glamour in shooting down a MiG than shooting up a SAM site.' But he added that missile and gun emplacements caused more concern for pilots than MiGs in the air.

Lt Phil Dempewolf also scored a probable with a Sidewinder on 21 July, although positive confirmation could not be made because two other MiGs attacked after Dempewolf's MiG went down.

Lt Cdr Robert Kirkwood became one of possibly two Crusader pilots who could claim a much-desired 'guns only' kill on this date, firing his 20 mm cannon at a MiG-17. Kirkwood was the leader of the second section flying TARCAP in F-8C BuNo 146992 (NP 424) for 15 A-4s. He had fired a Sidewinder at Isaack's MiG, but the XO's missile got there first. Kirkwood manoeuvred behind another MiG and fired another AIM-9. The target turned left as the Sidewinder exploded, and Kirkwood closed to gun range. At 600 ft he opened fire and the MiG went down.

Bob Kirkwood had the presence of mind to sit down and write the story of his engagement immediately after he returned to his ship. It appears here for the first time in print;

'We only saw the first four MiGs initially; the second four got behind us undetected. I lit my 'burner, put my nose on a MiG and selected a missile. In my excitement, I had buck fever, didn't wait for a tone, and fired. The missile went ballistic.

'I settled down a little, got a good, solid tone on another MiG and fired a second Sidewinder. But another F-8's missile got there first (Cdr Isaacks). There was another MiG, though, and after some gentle manoeuvring and 180° of turn, I fired a third missile. It ran hot and true, but after it detonated, the MiG was still flying. The pilot reversed his turn to the right. I cut him off and charged my guns. I was in good position, at his 6

Crewmen manoeuvre a VF-24 F-8C to its position on the flightdeck of *Bon Homme Richard* during the highly productive 1967 cruise

o'clock, and not pulling much G. I wanted to shoot from close in.

'I resisted the temptation to fire until I was at about 600 ft. I squeezed the trigger and closed to 300 ft. I could see my shells hitting the MiG's fuselage – patches of skin appeared to dissolve and bright, white fire seemed to fill the fuselage and leak out through the lacy skin.

'I broke left to avoid a collision, then dropped my right wing to look at the MiG. I didn't think there was much chance he would turn to attack me, but I couldn't turn my back on him. The pilot ejected after I passed him.'

After his successful engagement, Lt Cdr Kirkwood joined up with the rest of the F-8s as they headed back to their ship. At this point, Cdr Isaacks told Kirkwood that three-quarters of Kirkwood's starboard horizontal stabilator was missing. It had been shot away during the engagement. Kirkwood made a normal approach to his carrier, but the watchful LSO waved him off when he saw the missing stabilator. It was a tough, but necessary decision that would prevent the badly damaged Crusader from possibly crashing on the flight deck, thereby keeping the rest of the returning air wing from landing. After the rest of the carrier's aircraft had recovered, the LSO brought Kirkwood in for a normal landing.

Lt Cdr Tim Hubbard had been Jim Stockdale's LSO in VF-51 during those busy days of early August 1964. He now flew with VF-211 and had seen a lot of aerial action and several MiGs. He had hit a MiG with cannonfire, and the MiG had run, trailing smoke.

Today, his F-8E's (BuNo 150859) load-out included only one Sidewinder, along with Zunis, and he used both types of missiles, as well

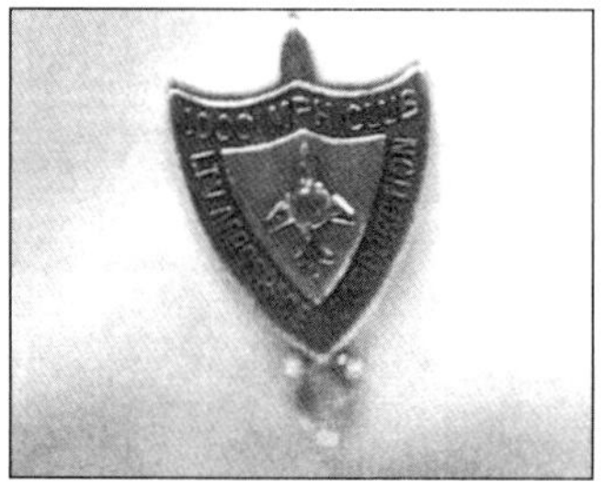

Part of a Crusader pilot's memorabilia – MiG-shooter Tim Hubbard's Vought jewellery includes two 1000-mph pins and an F-8 tie tack. The bottom pin is of interest because it carries a small ruby in the centre, denoting a MiG kill by the F-8 aviator. The latter is all the more unique considering that only 18 men received it (*via Mrs Johnnie Ann Hubbard*)

as 20 mm cannonfire, to down a MiG-17D. His kill raised his squadron's total to seven, making it the highest-scoring Navy unit at the time, and ultimately, the highest-scoring Crusader squadron.

When the MiG attacked his section, Hubbard made a hard, left turn into the threat, firing his cannon. Green tracers from behind told him he was under attack, and he turned hard again, forcing the second MiG to overshoot. Blasting away with his cannon, Hubbard decided to use all his weapons, but his single Sidewinder had not checked out before launch, so he fired two Zunis – coincidentally, he was escorting Lt Cdr T R Swartz of VA-76, who had scored a kill with Zunis over Kep on 1 May. During the debrief, Tim Hubbard learned that Swartz had gone to help 'Red' Isaacks, who was beset by a pack of MiG-17s. Swartz fired more Zunis at the enemy fighters, which quickly departed.

The big rockets required a huge lead angle, and the first salvo missed. Hubbard fired his remaining two Zunis, which blew up close enough to the MiG to cause major damage. After a few anxious moments, the North Vietnamese pilot ejected.

It was just payback as far as Hubbard was concerned. Exactly two months before on 21 May, Hubbard ejected from his F-8E (BuNo 150348 NP 105) while on approach to the *Bonnie Dick*. He had taken hits during a flak suppression run near Hanoi, the AAA striking his Crusader's afterburner section, but at first it didn't seem too bad and the aircraft was flyable. However, after refuelling in the air, and setting up for his recovery, raising his wing and dropping his landing gear, the F-8 burst into flame, forcing Hubbard to 'punch out'.

Tim Hubbard eventually became one of the most highly decorated Crusader 'drivers', garnering (besides the traditional Silver Star for his MiG kill) an incredible 16 DFCs and a Purple Heart, along with a profusion of Air Medals and campaign ribbons. His F-8E (150859) was lost – as an F-8J – in an operational mishap in 1970.

With 12 kills, CVW-21 was now the highest-scoring air wing. The Air Wing 21 cruise report (part of the massive amount of paperwork required by every combat deployment) attributed the wing's success against the MiGs to using the F-8s in their designed role – as fighters. This report summation denotes the radical deviation made by the air wing in contrast to others in respect to the employment of their F-8 aircraft. Wing bomb racks were never installed during the cruise. As a result, nine MiG-17s were confirmed shot down, plus one probable and nine more damaged in the air.

When air-to-ground ordnance was desired, the F-8s carried Zunis, mounted on the cheek missile stations. In certain cases, six Zunis and one AIM-9D were carried – F-8s in this configuration achieved two confirmed MiG kills.

The AIM-9D had largely supplanted the earlier -9B in F-8 squadrons by this time, and the change went a long way in improving the Crusader's tally. The -9B required nearly a dead-on tail shot, but the -9D offered greater launch parameters that the F-8 community used to advantage.

All the CVW-21 F-8 MiG killers received the Silver Star for their achievements, whilst Lt Dempewolf got the lesser Distinguished Flying Cross for his probable. Cdr Speer received the Navy Cross instead of the Silver Star, however, this being the second such award made to a VF-211 pilot. The Navy's highest award was made for his having 'contributed greatly to the successful execution of this mission' by protecting the A-4s from the determined enemy attack.

The Crusader had established its credentials as a MiG killer, and was eventually tagged by zealous public-relations officials as 'the MiG Master'.

The final US Navy MiG kill for 1967 was registered by a VF-162 F-8E. Lt Richard Wyman had launched from *Oriskany* (in BuNo 150879 AH 204) on 14 December as a 'spare'. Three other Crusaders had been scrubbed for mechanical reasons, and Wyman and Cdr CAL Swanson, who had assumed command of the 'Hunters' the year before, headed inland. Swanson's radar was down, and the lead fell to the junior pilot.

Cdr CAL Swanson during a post 1966-cruise visit to Pensacola. Named for pioneer aviator Charles Augustus Lindbergh, Swanson saw considerable action with VF-162 during his two tours with the 'Hunters', actually leading the squadron during its 1967-68 cruise

The pair spotted an A-4 from VA-164 with a VF-111 F-8 escort. The A-4 pilot, Lt(jg) Chuck Nelson, told them there were MiGs nearby as the F-8s closed on the fight. The MiGs were all over the lone 'Sundowner' F-8C, flown by Lt Cdr Dick Schaffert.

Schaffert's solo defence of the *Iron Hand* A-4 has become part of F-8 lore. Schaffert had only three of the usual four Sidewinders loaded, as the fourth missile hadn't checked out before launch, and was thus removed. Now he faced four aggressive MiG-17s alone, and help would be some time in coming;

'At one point, while I was pursuing the lead section of MiGs in a high-G, left turn, the second section got behind me. Tracers from the leader streaked over my canopy. The knee-jerk reaction to such a dire situation would have been to pull hard, putting on more Gs to "throw the shooter out of the saddle".

'However, I remembered an incident a few months before when MiG-17s had surprised two other VF-111 pilots by popping out of the clouds behind the F-8s. The Crusader pilots tried to out-turn the MiGs, which shot down one F-8 (the pilot was USAF exchange officer Capt Will Abbott – he was captured and spent the next six years as a PoW).

'Randy Rime took three cannon hits, one through the canopy, and he later made a spectacular wing-down recovered back aboard *Oriskany*.

'Realising I had little or no chance to escape by applying more Gs, I shoved the stick forward, abruptly going from six positive Gs to two negative Gs, while applying hard, left rudder to roll the nose under.

'The MiGs didn't follow that erratic manoeuvre, and I did a vertical reversal to meet them head-on. We later found with captured MiG-17s that they couldn't perform a negative-G roll without going "squirrely". It was the first time I had tried it in the F-8.'

The 'Hunter' flight arrived, and Cdr Swanson tried to manoeuvre with

Lt Cdr Dick Schaffert flew one of the legendary MiG engagements of the war, but in the end it was someone else who got the kill. Schaffert carries a 35 mm camera for chance shots for the intelligence department

VF-111 on board *Oriskany* in November 1967, this group shot showing a mixture of 'old hands' and new faces in comparison with the 'Sundowners' group shot seen earlier in this chapter. Back row, from left to right; Bob Rasmussen (CO), Jake Jacobsen, Craig Taylor, Dave Baker, Tom Garrett, Pete Peters, Carl Stattin and Jack Tinney (XO). Front row, from left to right; Dick Schaffert, Al Astin, Bob Jenkins, John Laughter, Jay Meadows, John Sande and Andy Anderson. CVW-16 suffered the highest losses of any air wing during the entire war on this cruise – with several high-level 'staffers' aboard, *Oriskany*'s aircraft led many Alpha strikes into heavily defended areas. The air wing was comprised of five squadrons, totalling 70 pilots and 60 aircraft, and between July 1967 and January 1968, it lost 37 aircraft and 26 pilots. On its previous cruise in 1966, CVW-16 had 33 pilots had been killed, six of which were listed as missing in action. Returning to VF-111, Lt(jg) Taylor was shot down on his first mission over Thanh Hoa, but was rescued – he was killed in a flight mishap at Miramar several months later. Lt(jg) Laughter earned the DFC during a mission over Hanoi, despite having only 150 hours in the F-8 at the time

one of the MiGs, but the North Vietnamese pilot got on his tail. Wyman shot a few bullets toward the MiG in an effort to save his skipper. Apparently, the MiG got the message and broke off. A dogfight developed. Each time Lt Wyman tried to fire a Sidewinder, the MiG would shake him off in a tight turn.

Another 'Sundowner' pilot, VF-111 CO Cdr Bob Rasmussen, who had been escorting a second A-4 on the same mission, was also in the fray. He had fired a Sidewinder at the MiG, but missed. The fight was now down to the trees – it had started at 16,000 ft. Finally, Wyman got behind the MiG and fired another Sidewinder. This time the AIM-9 guided perfectly and took off the MiG's left wing, the enemy fighter diving into the ground only 50 ft below.

The fight had shown there were good pilots on the other side, too. It had taken four F-8s, twisting and diving all over the sky, to bring down one MiG. Wyman recalled the climax of the long fight;

'The wing fell off. Red fire streaked along the left side of the plane as it cartwheeled into a rice paddy . . . This engagement was one of those intense, rare, moments in my life that fortunately culminated in an incredible high.'

Cal Swanson commented, 'That was probably the longest MiG engagement of the war. That MiG pilot was a tiger. He was there to fight'.

Dick Schaffert received a DFC for his incredible defence of the A-4s, but squadronmate Lt Cdr Pete Peters – who later became the first 3000-hour F-8 pilot – remarked dryly, 'Damn it, Dick. Four of those bastards to shoot at, and you didn't get any?'

MiGs were scarce for the next six months, at least for the Navy. The next kill did not come until June 1968, and, again, the victor was an F-8. Lt Cdr (later Rear Adm) L R Myers, operations officer for VF-51, was on his 182nd mission over Vietnam when used a Sidewinder to blow the tail off a MiG-21 on 26 June. The MiG made a head-on pass against the three VF-51 fighters, and Myers (he had been selected for commander) wrapped his Crusader (BuNo 148710 NF 116) into a turn, which put him at the MiG's six o'clock, and he fired his Sidewinder. It was the first of two kills for the F-8H model Crusader.

Lt Dick Wyman checks a Sidewinder missile. Wyman shot down a MiG-17 in December 1967 after one of the war's longest aerial engagements

VF-191's Lt Cdr John Nichols got the next kill in an engagement that graphically demonstrated why no RF-8s were lost to MiGs. On 9 July Nichols escorted an RF-8 on a low-level mission south of Vinh, the two *Ticonderoga* Crusaders drawing anti-aircraft fire throughout their run in toward the target.

Lt William Kocar brought his RF-8G down to 2000 ft, while Nichols remained at 3000 ft. As Kocar made his runs, Nichols spotted a camouflaged MiG-17 streaking toward the photo jet. Shouting a warning to Kocar and the controllers on the *Tico*, Nichols followed the RF-8 into a hard turn, just as tracers streamed past him – he had not seen the MiG's wingman.

Capt Dankworth (right), CO of *Bon Homme Richard*, congratulates Lt Cdr Myers after his MiG kill

Nichols focused on the lead MiG and fired a Sidewinder, but he was too high, and the missile did not guide properly. The MiG pilot suddenly stopped his turn, rolled wings level and lit his afterburner. Nichols saddled in and fired a second Sidewinder. This time the missile hit the MiG, causing major damage. The fighter remained in the air, however, much to Nichols' amazement, and he began firing his cannon, obtaining a few hits. The MiG was mortally wounded, and eventually disintegrated, Lt Kocar excitedly confirming the kill. Nichols' F-8E (BuNo 150926 NM 107) was also lost in an operational mishap in 1969 while flying from the *Oriskany* with VF-194.

After the Crusaders recovered aboard their carrier, the intelligence department presented Nichols with a biography of the young North Vietnamese pilot of the downed MiG. He had only about 450 hours total time, with 250 hours in the MiG-17 – 'Not a great deal, but it should have been enough to hack the programme with his initial advantage', Nichols later wrote.

Lt Cdr Nichols (right) is congratulated by his CO, Cdr Tuomela

On 27 July Lt Cdr Guy Cane, operations officer (and acting XO) of VF-53 in F-8E BuNo 150349 (NF 203), was leading four F-8Es that encountered a similar number of MiG-17s. Meeting a two-aircraft section head-on, Cane (who had been selected for commander) and his wingman, Lt(jg) Dexter Manlove, ended up turning with the enemy fighters until Cane got off a missile, which detonated just behind the MiG's tailpipe.

'I thought it had missed until a chunk of his starboard wing came off and the MiG went into a nosedown spiral', Cane later said. It was his 186th combat mission, and his first encounter with a MiG.

The Crusader's next kill followed only three days later. Again, it was a

Celebrating Lt Cdr Cane's victory. Left to right; Lt Cdr Cane, Lt Cdr Sandy Button, Lt(jg) Chuck Conrad and Lt Dexter Manlove (Cane's wingman)

photo-escort mission, or at least that's how it started. VF-51's Lt Norm McCoy was in an F-8H (BuNo 147916 NF 102), paired with Lt (later Rear Adm) Jay Miller in an RF-8G from VFP-63's Det 31. the photo dets were now designated by the hull number of the carrier to which they were assigned. Thus, Det 31 signified the *Bon Homme Richard*, CVA-31. Miller, on his second combat tour, had returned from a 1967 cruise in *Coral Sea* and had been assigned as the communications officer for VFP-63.

By the time of McCoy's kill, the Crusader units had lost several aeroplanes through operational attrition, which meant that they didn't always have enough jets to cover all the missions. What follows is Miller's account of Norm McCoy's MiG kill on 1 August;

'Norm was on a photo escort mission with me. There were probably two aeroplanes for either a BARCAP or FORCECAP between the boat and the beach. Usually, if things got out of sorts, the controllers just paired up who was left, and made a complete mission.

'George Hise was by himself. His "wingie" went down or something, and he was on his own. When Norm and I coasted out, after my mission, someone asked if my escort had enough gas to join Hise to take over the CAP mission.

'McCoy joined up with George and they got a vector toward a MiG from *Red Crown* – the radar-picket ship that watched for MiGs. I think there was also another section of F-8s from the *Intrepid* (these two Crusaders were led by Lt Tony Nargi from VF-111, who would go on to score the last official F-8 kill nearly ten months later), and they took out after

Representing the two fighter squadrons aboard *Bonnie Dick*, these two Crusaders are for VF-51 and VF-53. NF 102 (an F-8H) was flown by Lt McCoy during his MiG-killing engagement on 1 August 1968. NF 200 is an F-8E

the MiGs. Then McCoy and Hise got a vector, and for some reason the first section broke off, and Hise made contact and fired a missile. He called a hit. Within seconds after that, the MiG went into a cloud and the F-8s lost sight of him.'

Nargi's section had also found the fight, and a traditional 'fur ball' developed as the F-8 'drivers' lunged for the hapless MiG-21 pilot. Lt Miller continues;

MiG-shooters, all – Lt McCoy and Lt Hise tell Lt Cdrs Myers and Cane about their engagement

'When they re-acquired him, McCoy was in the driver's seat, close to a minute after Hise's call. He pickled off a 'winder and nailed him. Bang! Right there. Then, someone asked his state, and he came up with something ridiculous – 1400 or 1600 lbs. They gave him a tanker call, and he refused. He later told me he was following the MiG down taking pictures with his Super 8 movie camera mounted on his glare shield. He chased the MiG to the impact and got pictures of the smoke and flames. I think the MiG pilot ejected, but I'm not sure. When McCoy crossed the beach, he had about 800 lbs of fuel.

'He reached the A-3 tanker about 30 miles off the coast with about 400-500 lbs and plugged on the first shot. That always amazed me, because when you were just tanking for practice, it usually took you two tries, but it seemed every time you needed it, bang, it was always the first try – at least with the F-8 pilots.

'When we got back to the ship, the CAG listened to the tape of the kill I'd made in the plane and determined that since the MiG was still flying a full minute after Hise's hit – which apparently knocked off a piece of the MiG's wing – it was still manoeuvrable until McCoy's hit, which was fatal. He got the kill, but they both got to go to Saigon for the usual briefings that followed a kill.

The Crusader's last official Vietnam kill went to Lt Anthony J Nargi of VF-111's Det 11 whilst flying F-8C BuNo 146961 (AK 103) from the veteran 27C carrier *Intrepid*. The old ship had suffered a major *kamikaze* strike in 1945, and was now finishing its days as an anti-submarine carrier (CVS). During the escalated bombing campaign of 1966-68, it had been drafted to serve as a modified attack carrier with a small air wing.

Nargi and his wingman, Lt(jg) Alex Rucker (in F-8C BuNo 146955), were on a CAP mission on 19 September when they were

Lt(jg) Alex Rucker poses on his F-8C. In an unusual situation, the young F-8 pilot's brother Bill was also serving aboard the *Intrepid* during this cruise. Alex volunteered for the deployment when he learned that his brother was a communications officer in the old carrier

Lt Nargi with his wingman, Lt(jg) Rucker (right), with Cdr Thomas D Brown, XO of the *Intrepid*, after Nargi's MiG kill

alerted to incoming MiGs heading for their A-4 strike force. The two F-8s climbed to meet the threat, which turned out to be MiG-21s.

'I think the MiG pilot saw me about the same time', Nargi reported. 'I called', "MiG-21 high" to my wingman. The MiG pilot started taking evasive manoeuvres immediately. He climbed and went into a loop, and I was able to get into position behind him'. Nargi fired a Sidewinder, blowing the MiG's tail off, and the enemy fighter went down in a fireball. The North Vietnamese pilot ejected and floated down under an orange-and-white parachute.

Nargi and Rucker then engaged a second MiG. Both F-8 pilots fired missiles, which exploded close to the MiG, but the enemy jet seemed undamaged and quickly headed north to escape the VF-111 fighters. Nargi had scored the Navy's 29th MiG kill of the war, and the F-8's 18th, and last, confirmed victory.

Pickings were lean for the next three years, with only one Navy F-4 crew getting a kill in 1970. It was not until the heavy combat in the spring of 1972 that US crews began to score again, although the VPAF's maturing tactics and experience resulted in several periods of surprising success against Air Force Phantom IIs, whose crews still struggled with outdated combat formations and frustrating failures with the service's two primary aerial missiles, the AIM-4 Falcon and AIM-7 Sparrow – Air Force F-4s and the Navy's latest Sidewinder missile variant were not technically compatible.

On the *Hancock*'s LSO platform, Lt Tucker (with the telephone) works with two A-4 pilots to recover aircraft. Only the better naval aviators receive their CO's recommendation for LSO training, this position requiring the ability to observe, make quick decisions and endure exposure to every weather condition. It can also be one of the more dangerous spots to be on the flightdeck, itself one of the world's most hazardous work areas

Carrier-based Phantom II crews used their proven loose-deuce tactics and AIM-9 Sidewinders, as well as the highly touted training from the new Topgun school at Miramar, to shoot down 26 MiGs from 1970 to 1973 – they had scored 10 times during 1965-68. For the F-8, however, Nargi's kill represented the end of a relatively short list of victories. But that did not mean the Crusader's war was over.

There is, however, one last, controversial F-8 kill – that of VF-211's Lt Jerry Tucker on 23 May 1972. It wasn't as if the 'Checkmates' had nothing to do, for they had been quite busy supporting the intense war on the ground, delivering bombs and rockets against Communist positions in the face of occa-

Jerry Tucker's MiG 'scarer', NP 101, on a CAP mission in 1972

sionally intense flak and SAM defences. Still, every fighter pilot dreamt of at least one chance at a MiG . . .

The squadron now flew the F-8J, an upgraded 'Echo' that featured better avionics and boundary layer control, which improved the Crusader's notorious handling around the ship.

On this day, Tucker and Lt Cdr Frank Bachman were TARCAP for an Alpha strike near Vinh airfield. Orbiting their station was getting boring, and as the strikers returned, two of their F-4s from VF-161 got a vector toward a MiG that was coming out over the water in response to the attack on the airfield.

The two F-8 pilots listened to the proceedings as the F-4 crews quickly lost the 'bubble' and the MiG. Tucker called *Red Crown* and said *his* section was ready to go. *Red Crown* called the Phantom IIs off and sent the Crusaders toward the MiG.

Heading north, the F-8s spotted the MiG-17 and sped toward what seemed like a sure kill. Lt Tucker took the lead because he had the enemy fighter in sight. The MiG was low and really moving out. Tucker's Sidewinder began to growl, indicating the missile's seeker head was 'sniffing' its quarry.

Suddenly, the MiG's canopy flew off, followed by the pilot. Tucker watched incredulously as his 'kill' floated down under a white parachute. The frustrated Crusader pilot made two passes by the understandably nervous North Vietnamese pilot, whose head turned as the American fighter flashed past him.

Unfortunately, the Navy denied credit for the kill, leaving those concerned, as well as historians, to argue the point for posterity. One of the aspects of this 'engagement' has long been whether the MiG pilot punched out when he found his opponents were F-8s instead of F-4s. Of course, the Crusader 'drivers' will say that his reaction was understandable given the potent reputation of the F-8. As Lt Tucker points out, however, only *that* MiG pilot knows for sure, and he has long since faded into the security of anonymity.

ASSESSING THE ENEMY

Throughout the war, US airmen duelled with the small VPAF, and although the North Vietnamese had been sending their pilot trainees to the Soviet Union and Communist China since the late 1950s, their complement of modern jet fighters remained small until the 1970s. The USSR sent 36 MiG-17s to bolster the meagre number of obsolescent MiG-15s in 1963, and the VPAF duly stood up the 921st Fighter Regiment. A few twin-engine MiG-19s also appeared in 1972, serving with the 925th Fighter Regiment – the 'MiGs' were actually Chinese-built J-6 copies.

Top-of-the-line MiG-21s arrived in 1965 to re-equip the 921st, whose MiG-17s in turn helped form the new 923rd Fighter Regiment. However, the MiG-21s were only occasionally committed to battle in the next two years following their first appearance on 23 April 1966, when they lost a MiG to USAF F-4s. The main burden of the confrontations with the Americans therefore fell to the MiG-17 units that staged from the growing number of airfields up and down the length of North Vietnam.

At the time of the Gulf of Tonkin Incident in August 1964, the VPAF had only one major airfield, at Phuc Yen, north-west of Hanoi. By 1968, however, three more major airfields – Kep, Gia Lam (the country's main commercial airport) and Yen Bai – and three emergency strips were operating MiGs.

VPAF pilots were, for the most part, young and inexperienced, lacking in much of the intense training their counterparts in the US Navy, Marine Corps and Air Force took for granted. In some respects, the rural upbringing of many of the VPAF MiG pilots also worked against them, leaving them relatively unfamiliar with machinery more complicated than a bicycle. However, the North Vietnamese pilots were enthusiastic and eager to learn, even if the learning came at the price of losing many of their compatriots to the F-4s and F-105s that flew over their homeland in increasing numbers.

In respect to shooting down American aircraft, the prize seemed to be the F-8. It would appear that the VPAF eagerly claimed as destroyed a number of Navy Crusaders that definitely recovered either aboard their ship or at least ashore at Da Nang.

American records attribute the loss of just three F-8s directly to MiGs – all in 1966 – throughout the

In a scene repeated many times in the war, North Vietnamese peasants (some armed) inspect the wreckage of Lt(jg) C P Zuhoski's F-8C (BuNo 146894) in a Hanoi suburb. The VF-111 fighter was hit by a SAM on 31 July 1967, its young pilot ejecting and being captured (*VPAF via Dr Zoltan Buza and Istvan Toperzer*)

eight-year war, although a few were so badly damaged upon making it home that they were scrapped. Thus, for those who enjoy 'working' the figures, the 6:1 ratio usually quoted for the Crusader regarding kills to losses (18 official MiGs downed by F-8s versus 3 F-8s lost to MiGs), can be drastically modified to 4.5:1 or less. Seven MiG-killing Crusaders were eventually lost, three being shot down by flak, one so badly shot up after its MiG engagement that it was struck of charge and three written off in operational mishaps.

A MiG-17 'Fresco C' launches on an intercept mission in 1968, possibly from Gia Lam Airport. Derived from the Korean War MiG-15, the MiG-17 was a good fighter for the small VPAF, which initially boasted only limited expertise and support. US crews respected the MiG's turning ability and heavy cannon. Note the national insignia, which markedly resembles that of the US armed forces

The question of whether more than three F-8s were downed by MiGs is still open to interpretation. The VPAF claims as many as 13 F-8 kills, beginning in April 1965. However, it is a fact that all the VF-211 F-8Es involved in this encounter recovered either aboard ship, or in one case, ashore at Da Nang. Like every generation of combat aviators, in the heat of the action the youthful MiG 'drivers' mistook smoke and ruptured metal as confirmation of a kill, instead of a lesser degree of damage which allowed the US aircraft to make it home.

HOW MANY KILLS?

Confusion also developed over several F-8 aviators' possible second kills – as well as those of the USAF – partly perhaps because the US armed forces did not want to publicise that it listened in on VPAF frequencies. It is likely that in the case of Hal Marr's second kill (listed officially as a 'probable'), Navy controllers learned that the MiG was destroyed, possibly when its pilot ejected, or perhaps when a so-called 'hill watcher' reported in with the news. Whatever the case, after more than 30 years it is well known that the Americans did monitor enemy radio transmissions – there is nothing wrong with that, especially during wartime – and that a network of in-country observers kept tabs on what aircraft went down.

Therefore, the time has come to give Hal Marr his justly deserved credit for a second kill. Shortly after the event a staff member at Pearl Harbor told the VF-211 CO that the kill was confirmed, but would not be credited to protect the source of the confirmation – probably a 'hill-watcher'.

Although the problem is not new in combat aviation, there are other F-8 MiG-killers such as Phil Wood and Tim Hubbard who probably also have additional victories which are only officially listed as 'probables'. As now-retired Capt Wood opined, 'Only the "hill watchers" know for sure'. If, as in Hal Marr's case, the knowledge is more definite, these men deserve an extra effort from the Navy to finally credit them with their second kills.

For all the effort and time the US armed forces occasionally take to award servicemen from World War 2 their Medal of Honor (certainly justly deserved even at this late date), surely a few days' time to corroborate facts from 30 years ago would not be amiss. The "hill-watchers" near Hanoi and Haiphong can't be the only ones who know the truth.

A typical view on a communist airfield shows three VPAF MiG-21PF pilots strolling along the flightline, perhaps discussing their flight tactics against the Americans. They wear G-suits, the Soviet-style helmet with exterior-mounted visors and, one supposes, the Soviet equivalent of the flight jacket. Their 'Fishbed Ds' carry 'Atoll' air-to-air missiles – copies of pirated Sidewinders

By the same token, it is understandable if Navy public affairs officers, working off the debriefings of their tired and excited aviators, did not want to admit to more than a few Crusader losses to MiGs. If an F-8 did not return, and the reason was not clear-cut, then the Crusader loss was usually attributed to flak or a SAM, not to an enemy fighter pilot.

VPAF ACES

Some material about the VPAF and its top pilots is beginning to appear in print, as well as in enthusiasts' private logs. The long-running discussion about whether the VPAF's top ace, 'Colonel Tomb', actually existed may at last have been resolved to an extent.

There were several skilled VPAF pilots, and there appears to have been at least a dozen aces created flying red-starred MiGs. The top scorer – Capt Nguyen Van Coc – is credited with nine kills, whilst several pilots claimed five (Coc now commands the VPAF as a major general). As for the enigmatic 'Col Tomb', he might have been a MiG-21 pilot named 'Ton', whose name was mispronounced or misspelled by western, particularly American, journalists. As one recent correspondent averred, 'Tomb was much more dramatic'. 'Ton' seems to have been a 'cell name' – somewhat akin to a call sign – given to Nguyen Hong Nhi, an eight-kill ace (Capt Nguyen Van Coc's moniker might have been 'Bieu').

Apparently Ton was killed in action on 10 May 1972, but not in the MiG-17/F-4 engagement with sole US Navy aces Lt Randy Cunningham and Lt(jg) Willie Driscoll. The VF-96 aviators *did* go up against a capable MiG-17 pilot, who simply ran out of luck and gas, but it was not 'Tomb' or Ton, who did not fly the older MiG. It seems that VF-92's Lt Curt Dose and Lt Cdr Jim McDevitt shot down Ton's MiG-21 over Kep Airfield on the morning of 10 May 1972 just as the VPAF ace launched to intercept a US raid – four hours *before* the engagement involving Cunningham and Driscoll.

As with many little-known air forces – especially those of Asian countries – the tendency has been to denigrate the capabilities of VPAF pilots. But if there were many young MiG pilots who went into combat with barely 500 hours total time, there was a cadre of experienced, aggressive, aviators who met the F-8 and F-4 crews on a more equal footing. Some day their story will be fully told.

Nguyen Van Bay was a MiG-17 ace. Besides having participated in the surprising series of raids in 1972 against US ships, he may also have been the pilot – usually, but incorrectly, identified as 'Col Tomb' – shot down by VF-96's ace pairing of Randy Cunningham and Willie Driscoll on 10 May 1972 as their third kill of the day. Wearing the trademark cloth helmet and goggles of the MiG pilot, he also displays seven 'Uncle Ho' badges, one for each of his victories

BEYOND THE MiGS

Young Lt Jerry Weber was having a hard day. Having joined VF-53 barely six months before, he was a 'nugget' trying to hang onto his flight leader, Lt Rick Harris, as they diverted to Da Nang after an uneventful BARCAP off Haiphong on 24 March 1968.

Weather had prevented the two Crusader pilots from recovering aboard *Bon Homme Richard*, and although conditions ashore weren't much better, at least Da Nang wasn't pitching and rolling. Weber's radio and Tacan had gone out, and it was up to Lt Harris to lead his flight to a safe landing.

Struggling to keep up with Harris, Weber followed the other F-8 into the undercast as they began their descent. The rain was heavy in the thick clouds, and Weber gave his complete attention to focusing on his leader. Suddenly, there was a flash of green in his peripheral vision and he began hitting trees. He tried pulling up, but the damaged engine would not respond, and the F-8 began rolling. Weber pulled the face curtain, leaving his Crusader (BuNo 150306) to crash into the ground near the Marine Corps facility at Da Nang's Monkey Mountain.

For the next two hours, the young aviator spent many anxious moments as he tried collecting himself and his gear. He was not sure where he was, and Viet Cong rebels were still active in the jungles surrounding South Vietnam's population centres.

VF-53 in 1967. Cdr Paul Gillcrist (CO) is fourth from right in the rear row, whilst Lt Jerry Weber is in the front row at the extreme right

The remains of F-8E BuNo 150306 of VF-53 on 12 March 1968. Its young pilot, Lt Jerry Weber, had ejected after trying to land at Da Nang

Crewmen begin jettisoning bombs overboard during the *Oriskany* fire. Here, they hurl a bomb off the starboard sponson, just outboard and aft of the compartment where the fire began

He had hit trees as he descended in his 'chute, and he was scratched and bruised. He was also very thirsty. Using his personal survival radio, he was finally able to contact a helicopter whose crew was looking for him. Low on fuel, however, they had to leave. 'The loneliest feeling I have ever felt came over me then', Weber recalls. When another helicopter appeared, he fired a signal flare. The helo crew arrived and lowered a jungle penetrator – a device with a seat that could get through the incredibly dense canopy.

After a medical examination at Da Nang, Jerry Weber was reunited with his contrite flight leader. Harris explained he had been trying to get the flight back above the cloud layer, but that they had hit a ridgeline at 1100 ft.

Three months later on 25 June Jerry Weber had to eject again, this time at night over the Gulf of Tonkin. Flying F-8E BuNo 149158, he tried to refuel from an A-4 tanker, but something was wrong and he couldn't take on any gas. Although he wanted to divert to Da Nang, his CO adamantly told him to recover back aboard ship. As he desperately tried again to refuel, Weber's engine flamed out, and once more he found himself hanging from a 'chute, this time headed for the dark water of the Gulf. Sharks were known to frequent the area.

He was eventually retrieved, but as he waited patiently for rescue, he

Right
The 'Superheats' of VF-162 in 1967. Front row, from left to right; Ron Thurman, Jim Shaw, John McDonald, Bob Aumack (XO), CAL Swanson (CO), Butch Verich, Stu Harrison, John Hellman, Bob Walters and Tom Dallas. Rear row, from left to right; Jack Jeffords, Jim Brady, Ron Coalson, Dick Wyman, J P O'Neill, Rich Minnich, Ray Leach, Lea Fernandez, Blair Edwards, Bob Punches, Pat Crahan and Jim Woodward. Lt(jg) Minnich was killed in action on this cruise, while Lt Cdr Verich was shot down for the second time and sent home. Cdr Aumack was a former Blue Angel who replaced Cdr Hunter, who was killed trying to bring his damaged aircraft back to the ship. Dick Wyman became the 'Hunters'' second MiG killer soon after this photo was taken (NMNA)

swears something bumped against him in the darkness several times.

Although MiG kills always grabbed the headlines, there were many other mundane aspects to the F-8 pilot's combat career – living in a squadron, and just surviving a six-month deployment (35-day line periods on 'Yankee Station' were not rare), which could sometimes last longer. CAL Swanson calculated that a MiG was seen perhaps once in every 200 missions. 'It seemed like an awful lot of exposure to ground fire, flak and SAMs for not putting much hurt on the enemy', he said.

Lt Cdr Schaffert of VF-111 commented, 'By the end of the 1967-68 cruise (aboard *Oriskany*) we were a 'salty' outfit. Even with seven 'nuggets', we averaged more than 800 hours per pilot in the Crusader, with more than 100 combat missions'.

How it looked from another ship. Smoke pours from *Oriskany* as crewmen seek the relative safety and open air of the flightdeck

Fully armed with four Sidewinders, this VF-51 F-8E prepares to launch from USS *Hancock* in 1967 during the only combat cruise the 'Screaming Eagles' made aboard 'the Handjob'

A striking photo of Lt(jg) Chuck Rice's F-8E (BuNo 150310) being hit by 85 mm AAA on 26 October 1967 during a strike on Hanoi. Happily, although his friends were sure he hadn't survived such a disastrous hit, the VF-162 pilot returned with other PoWs in 1973. VA-163's Lt (now-Senator) John McCain was also shot down and imprisoned on this mission, his A-4E (BuNo 149959 AH 300) having been struck by a SAM

There were a lot of characters in *Oriskany*'s Air Wing 16, but they had earned their colourful reputation for CVW-16 had suffered the worst losses of the war. The air wing led many Alpha strikes against intense enemy opposition. With a normal complement of five squadrons, 70 pilots and 60 aircraft, CVW-16 lost 37 aircraft and 26 pilots from July 1967 to January 1968. On the previous cruise in 1966, the wing had lost no fewer than 33 pilots, including six men who were listed as missing in action.

Many of the 1966 complement also experienced the *Oriskany* fire of 26 October 1966, one of three conflagrations that occurred on three different carriers during the war – the other fires were on USS *Forrestal* (CVA-59) in July 1967 and USS *Enterprise* (CVAN-65) in January 1969. While all these tragic events consumed many lives, *Oriskany*'s fire was especially preventable as it started with the lackadaisical (albeit not criminal) actions of two young sailors toting signal flares.

Amongst Air Wing 16's losses were many pilots, including the air wing commander – Cdr Bellinger of VF-162 was tapped to fill in. A personal account of one man's experience in the fire is featured in the companion volume on RF-8s.

Dick Schaffert's stateroom was only 20 ft from the locker where the flares ignited, and his roommate, Norm Levy, did not survive the fire. Schaffert also spoke on the phone with his wingman, Lt(jg) Bill McWilliams, and three other junior pilots – the area around them was flooded, and there was no hope of rescue before their air ran out.

CAL Swanson, then XO of VF-162, saved himself and 13 other men by taking them down into the burning ship and finding refuge in a vertical trunk on the second deck. After

COLOUR PLATES

This colour section profiles the F-8s flown by 16 MiG killers, plus other Vietnam-period Crusaders of note. All the artwork has been specially commissioned for this volume, and profile artist Tom Tullis and figure artist Mike Chappell have gone to great pains to illustrate the aircraft, and their pilots, as accurately as possible following exhaustive research by the author. All of the Crusaders depicted on the following pages have never been illustrated in colour before, and the schemes shown have been fully authenticated either by the pilot(s) who flew the aircraft in combat, or from contemporary photographs taken by the US Navy/Marine Corps or naval aviators serving during the Vietnam War.

1

F-8E BuNo 150924 NP 103 of Cdr Harold L Marr, CO of VF-211, USS *Hancock*, 12 June 1966

2

F-8E BuNo 150300 NP 104 of Lt(jg) Phillip V Vampatella, VF-211, USS *Hancock*, 21 June 1966

3

F-8E BuNo 149159 AH 210 of Cdr Richard M Bellinger, CO of VF-162, USS *Oriskany*, 9 October 1966

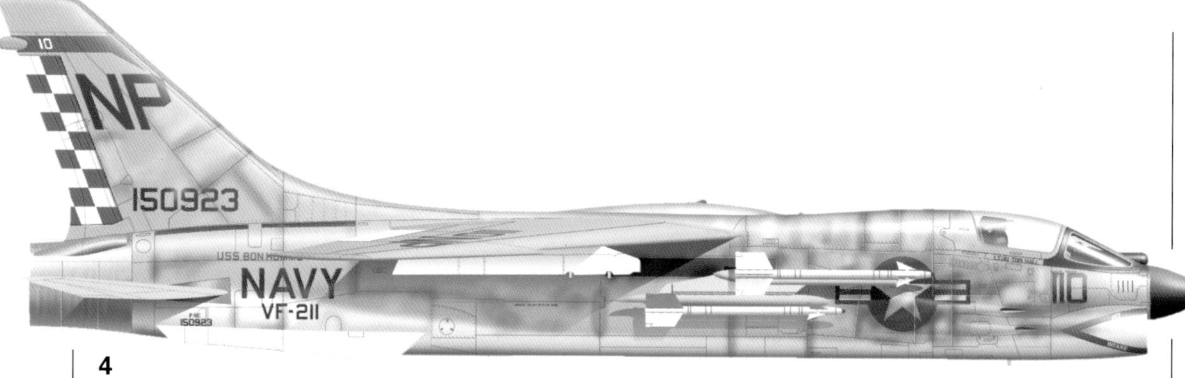

4

F-8E BuNo 150923 NP 110 of Lt Cdr Marshall O 'Mo' Wright, VF-211, USS *Bon Homme Richard*, 1 May 1967

5

F-8E BuNo 150661 NP 102 of Lt(jg) Joseph M Shea, VF-211, USS *Bon Homme Richard*, 19 May 1967

6

F-8C BuNo 147029 NP 443 of Lt Phillip R Wood, VF-24, USS *Bon Homme Richard*, 19 May 1967

7

F-8C BuNo 147018 NP 442 of Cdr Marion H 'Red' Isaacks, VF-24, USS *Bon Homme Richard*, 21 July 1967

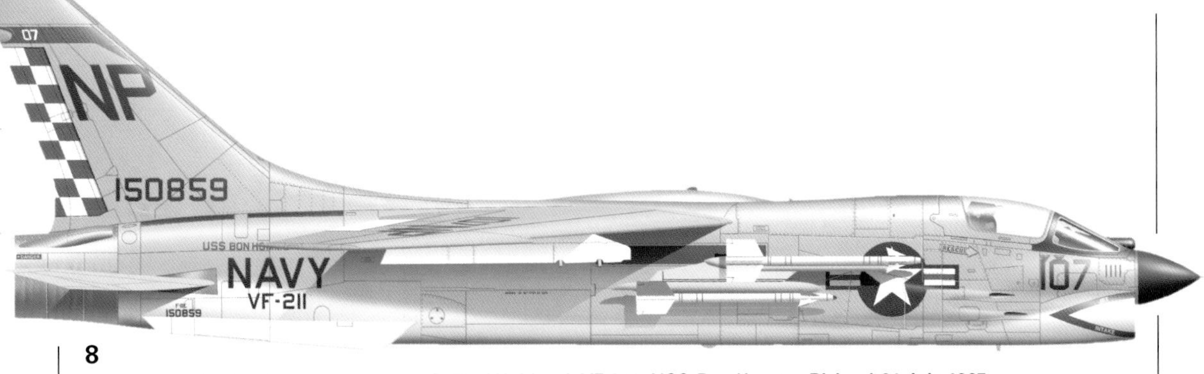

8

F-8E BuNo 150859 NP 107 of Lt Cdr Ray G 'Tim' Hubbard, VF-211, USS *Bon Homme Richard*, 21 July 1967

9

F-8C BuNo 146992 NP 447 of Lt Cdr Robert L Kirkwood, VF-24, USS *Bon Homme Richard*, 21 July 1967

10

F-8E BuNo 150879 AH 204 of Lt Richard E Wyman, VF-162, USS *Oriskany*, 14 December 1967

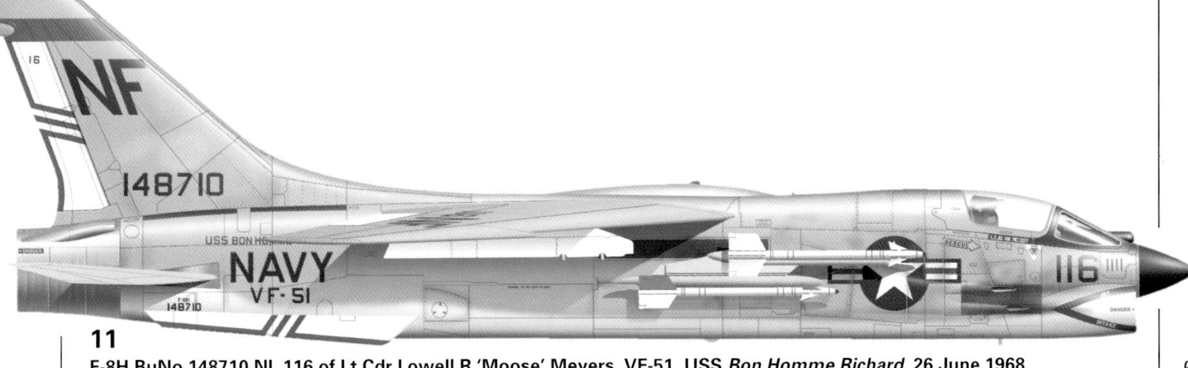

11

F-8H BuNo 148710 NL 116 of Lt Cdr Lowell R 'Moose' Meyers, VF-51, USS *Bon Homme Richard*, 26 June 1968

12

F-8E BuNo 150926 NM 101 of Lt Cdr John B Nichols III, VF-191, USS *Bon Homme Richard*, 9 July 1968

13

F-8E BuNo 150349 NF 203 of Lt Cdr Guy Cane, VF-53, USS *Bon Homme Richard*, 29 July 1968

14

F-8H BuNo 147916 NF 102 of Lt Norman K McCoy, VF-51, USS *Bon Homme Richard*, 1 August 1968

15

F-8C BuNo 146961 AK 103 of Lt Anthony J Nargi, VF-111, USS *Intrepid*, 9 September 1968

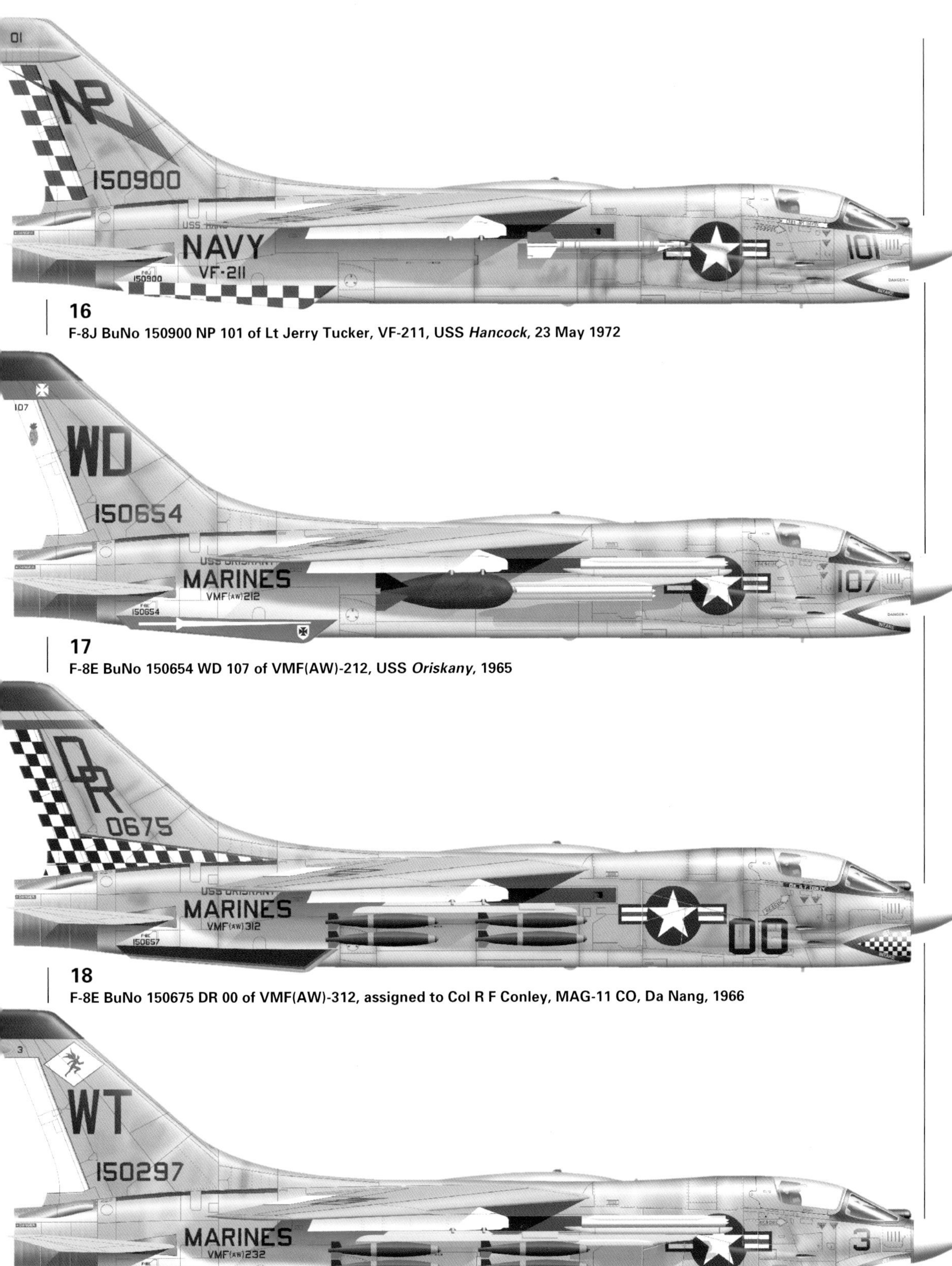

16

F-8J BuNo 150900 NP 101 of Lt Jerry Tucker, VF-211, USS *Hancock*, 23 May 1972

17

F-8E BuNo 150654 WD 107 of VMF(AW)-212, USS *Oriskany*, 1965

18

F-8E BuNo 150675 DR 00 of VMF(AW)-312, assigned to Col R F Conley, MAG-11 CO, Da Nang, 1966

19

F-8E BuNo 150297 WT 3 of VMF(AW)-232, MAG-12, Da Nang, 1966

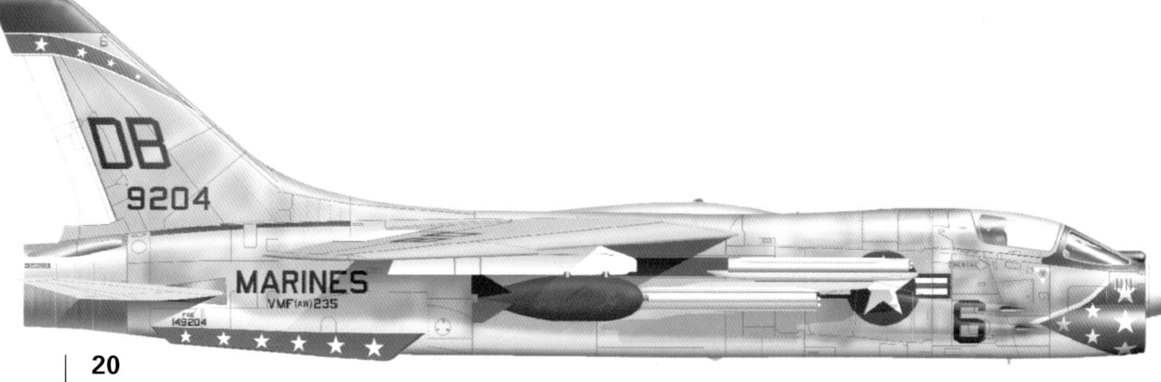

20
F-8E BuNo 149204 DB 6 of VMF(AW)-235, MAG-12, Da Nang, 1967

21
DF-8D BuNo 143738 UE 1 of VC-5, Da Nang, 1965

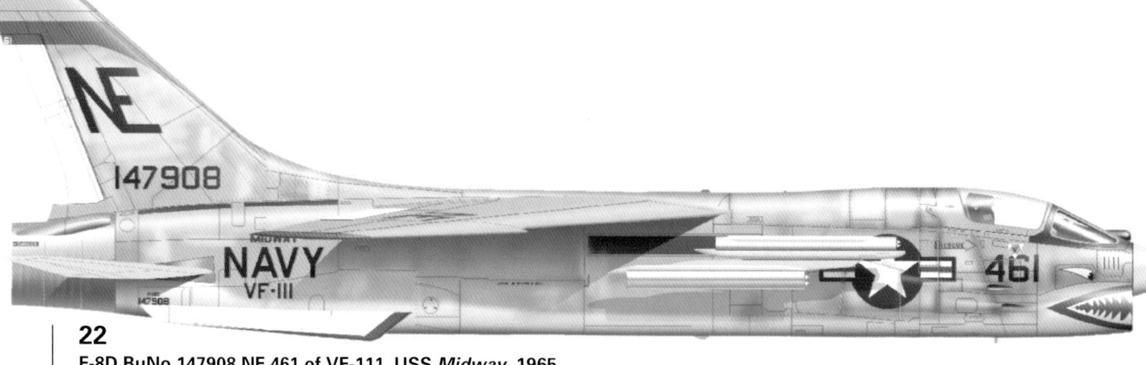

22
F-8D BuNo 147908 NE 461 of VF-111, USS *Midway*, 1965

23
F-8D BuNo 148673 NL 413 of VF-154, USS *Coral Sea*, 1965

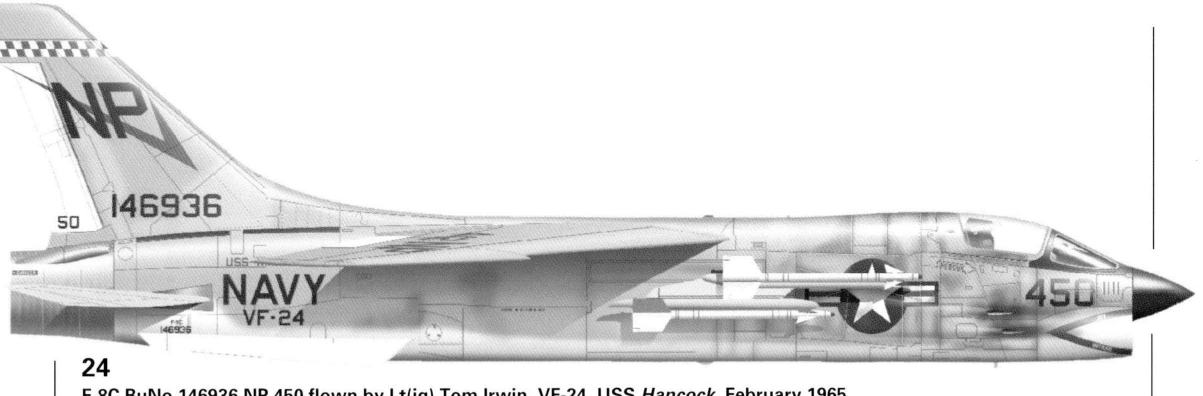

24
F-8C BuNo 146936 NP 450 flown by Lt(jg) Tom Irwin, VF-24, USS *Hancock*, February 1965

25
F-8E BuNo 148178 NF 101 of Cdr James Stockdale, CO of VF-51, USS *Ticonderoga*, August 1964

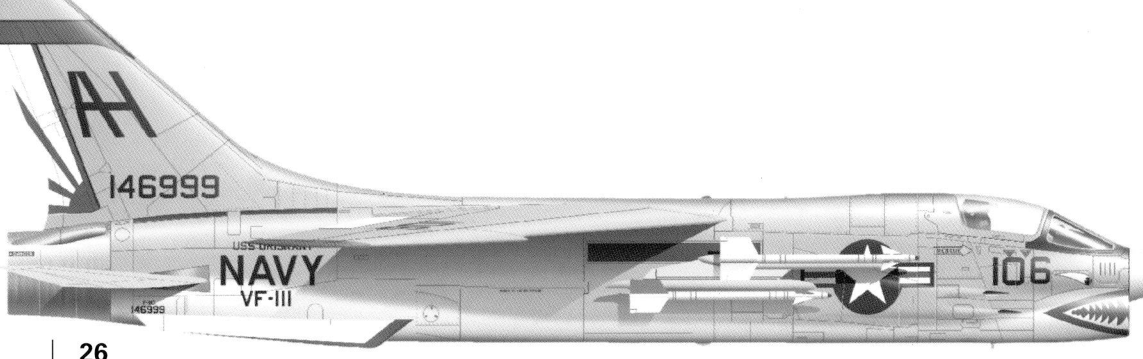

26
F-8C BuNo 146999 AH 106 of Lt Cdr Dick Schaffert, VF-111, USS *Oriskany*, 14 December 1967

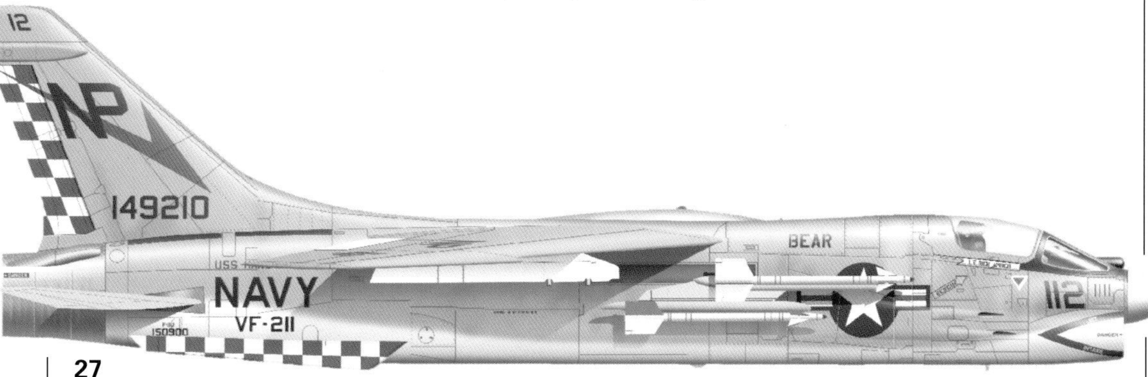

27
F-8J BuNo 149210 NP 112 of Lt Rick Amber, VF-211, USS *Hancock*, January 1971

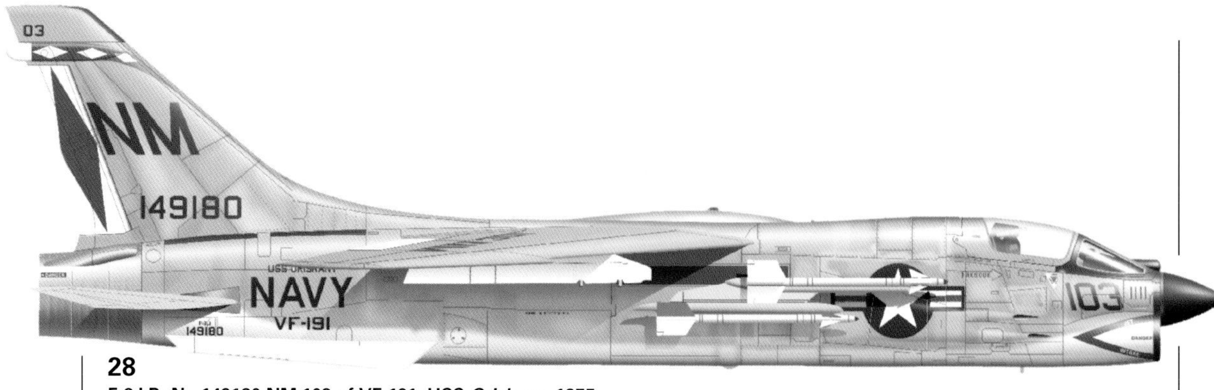

28

F-8J BuNo 149180 NM 103 of VF-191, USS *Oriskany*, 1975

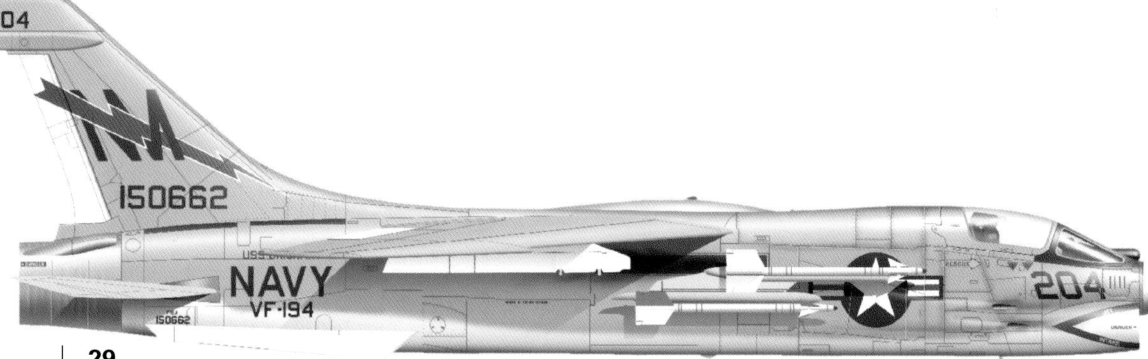

29

F-8J BuNo 150662 NM 204 of VF-194, USS *Oriskany*, 1975

30

F-8E BuNo 149199 NF 211 of Lt Jerry A Weber, VF-53, USS *Bon Homme Richard*, 1967

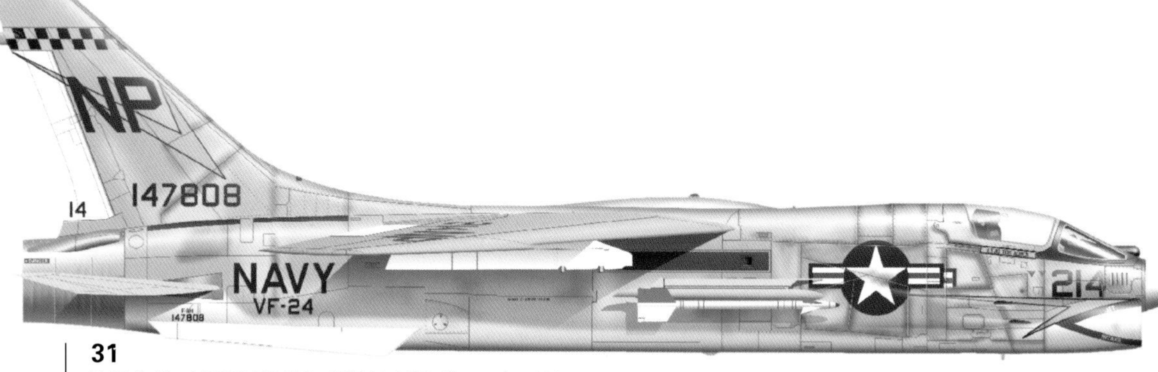

31

F-8H BuNo 147908 NP 214 of VF-24, USS *Hancock*, 1969

32
F-8E BuNo 150900 NF 234 of VF-53, USS *Ticonderoga*, 1965

33
F-8E BuNo 150900 NF 209 of VF-53, USS *Hancock*, 1967

1
Lt(jg) Phil Vampatella of VF-211, sailing in USS *Hancock*, June 1966

2
Cdr James B Stockdale, CO of VF-51, sailing in USS *Ticonderoga*, August 1964

3
Cdr Dick Bellinger, CO of VF-162 sailing in USS *Oriskany*, October 1966

4
Lt Cdr Richard Schaffert of VF-111, sailing in USS *Oriskany*, December 1967

5
Capt Peter 'Drax' Williams of VMF(AW)-235 at Da Nang in 1968

6
Lt Dudley Moore of VF-194 at NAS Miramar, California, between combat cruises aboard USS *Ticonderoga* in 1966-67

WHEN YOU'RE OUT OF F-8's
YOU'RE OUT OF FIGHTERS
232

1

2

3

NE
461
147908
NAVY
VF-111

4

5

6

7

8

9

10A

10B

11

12

13

14

15

16

17

18

19

two-and-a-half hours Swanson contacted a repair team, which pulled out the more seriously injured of his group. Swanson then led the remaining people to safety.

When *Oriskany* was repaired and ready for another deployment in April 1967, Swanson was now the CO of the 'Hunters'. At one point there were not enough F-8Es for both VF-111 and VF-162, and in a somewhat arbitrary decision, the admiral at Miramar re-assigned the available 'Echoes' to the 'Sundowners' and gave F-8Cs to VF-162 – much to the consternation of the new 'Hunter' skipper. Swanson argued that his unit was much more experienced in ground attack, and thus should have the F-8Es and their hardpoint wings. The admiral reconsidered, then flipped a coin, which landed in favour of the 'Hunters'!

At this time the most common bomb was the Mk 82 500-lb iron bomb. However, there was a large arsenal of World War 2-era Mk 60 bombs still in storage awaiting use, the latter weapon being distinguished by its more rotund appearance in comparison with the modern Mk 82 series. Fitted with fuse extenders, the Mk 60s proved to be good flak-suppressors.

'We had varying success with cluster bombs for flak suppression', Swanson recalls. 'It was tricky using them because you had to be right on flight parameters to get a good ground pattern.'

On one occasion Swanson and his wingman, Bob Punches, were on a flak-suppression mission with Mk 65 'daisy-cutter' weapons. The weather over the primary target was bad, so Swanson led his flight on an armed reconnaissance of a river south-west of Haiphong.

Unable to find any barges on the river, the two F-8 'drivers' turned their attention to a bridge. In a shallow, ten-degree dive, the CO 'pickled' his four bombs. But he had forgot to arm them, and the bombs didn't drop. Chagrined, he came around for another run. This time, the bombs

Enlisted crewmen tow AK 105 (an F-8C) around the *Intrepid*'s hangar bay.

dropped next to the bridge, triggering a secondary explosion. His wingman now made his delivery and got direct hits on the bridge.

When they returned to their ship and debriefed, the two 'Hunter' pilots discovered the bridge 'belonged' to an A-4 pilot of VA-163, who had made it his personal target for several days!

Other targets during the cruise included trains, which proved susceptible to Zunis and even Sidewinders. Once, CAL Swanson and his flight happened upon a North Vietnamese train that was under attack by A-4s. The 'Scooter' pilots had used up all their ordnance and ammunition and invited the Crusader pilots to try their collective hand. Only too happy to oblige, Swanson and his men descended on the hapless little locomotive, firing their Sidewinders. The aerial missiles hit the engine right in its boiler with appropriate results.

VF-162 lost five aircraft in combat and two in operational mishaps during this cruise, two pilots being killed in action and one captured. Swanson was the only aviator in the entire wing who served full tours as XO and CO.

On 19 July 1967 Swanson lost his XO, Herb Hunter, whose F-8 (BuNo 150899 AH 206) had suffered several hits in the wing and fuselage during a mission. Struggling to reach *Oriskany* with bombs he could not jettison, Hunter closed on *Bon Homme Richard*, which was closer and was recovering aircraft.

Swanson was in *Oriskany*'s tower, but because the two carriers were too far apart for communications, he couldn't switch to the other carrier's frequency as his XO set up for a landing on a strange ship. Thus, Swanson and his men had to learn later that Hunter couldn't raise his Crusader's wing (a vital part of the landing sequence), which meant he would touch down at a much higher speed than normal. A former Blue Angel, Hunter was settling much faster than normal, and he hit the deck so hard that all three of his landing gear collapsed as his tailhook failed to hold onto the arresting wire it had grabbed. Hunter's aircraft slid off the carrier's angled deck and into the water, taking its pilot with it.

'Herb was one of the best pilots I have ever known', Swanson said, 'and he was confident in his ability to deal with the vagaries of the Crusader'.

Bob Aumack took Hunter's place as XO.

One of the most colourful characters in a world of such people was Lt Joseph Satrapa. Flying with VF-111's F-8C Det 11 on board *Intrepid* in 1968, he flew missions that ran the gamut, all with a particular élan that still leaves people shaking their heads at the mention of his name. His original call sign was 'Roadrunner', but it was later changed to 'Hoser', to which name he still answers.

Intrepid's air wing was what could charitably be called 'an experiment'. Too small to host the normal-sized wing, the old World War 2 carrier had room for three squadrons of A-4s (VA-36, VA-66, and VA-106) and a detachment of VF-111 F-8Cs, a detachment of RF-8Gs of VFP-63, a det of VAQ-33 EA-1Fs and a detachment of E-1Bs of VAW-121. The summer of 1968 was a hectic time in the South China Sea, as 'Hoser' Satrapa relates;

'I was known as kind of a wild guy, and they figured I needed someone to keep me company. So I was wingman for "Tooter" Teague, the det OINC.

Lt Joe Satrapa pre-flights his Crusader's ejection seat before strapping in for a mission in 1968. Note the leg garters just below his knees, the pilot threading a cloth-covered line through the buckles of the garters as he settled into his seat. He then connected the loose end of the line into the base of his seat. If he had to eject, the line instantly pulled his legs against the seat to keep them from flailing during the ride up the rails

'Our job was primarily MiGCAP, TARCAP and photo escort. The BARCAP mission was given to the larger-deck ships with the F-4s, which was great, because the chances for a hot MiG vector on BARCAP were very remote.

'We'd escort the A-4s in. They'd be jinking at 16,000-18,000 ft to confuse the folks on the ground. Approaching the beach, we'd set up a big 450-500-knot weave across the top of them, 3000-4000 ft above, checking for MiGs. The MiGs' favourite tactic was popping up from below. As we crossed the beach I would go through my combat checklist: droops up, or by 450 knots, Sidewinder selected cold/on, G-suit plugged in, ALE-39 chaff dispenser on, ALQ-100 ECM interrogator on for ECM signals. And press on.

'Once we hit the Thanh Hoa railroad yard. "Snuffy" Smith was the A-4 strike leader, and I was flying TARCAP. As we crossed over the beach about 12 miles south of the Thanh Hoa Bridge, we could see the smoke pots on the bridge that the "gomers" put there to smudge the bridge so that our Walleye missiles wouldn't work.

'We worked the railyard over real good. We could see box cars flying and turning over. Lot of SAMs. Four days later, we went directly against the bridge, which was always a prime target. This time, they didn't have the smoke pots on the bridge because they thought we were coming back to the railyard.

A characteristic view during underway replenishment in July 1968. The three F-8 tails display many insignias, the VF-111 F-8C at the extreme left showing the squadron's 'Sundowner' markings. BuNo 145632 is an RF-8G, while BuNo 146951 is assigned to Lt(jg) Alex Rucker, call sign 'Rattler'

'The A-4s went in, and made a big SAM break. With all their Mk 82s, they were forced down into the flak envelope. The AAA was awesome. If you got hit with a piece of the flak shell after it burst, it could do just as much damage as a direct hit.

'"Snuffy" Smith cut loose with a Walleye and got the southern span of the bridge. He got a Silver Star for that. The Thanh Hoa area, aside from the Hanoi-Haiphong, was probably the most heavily defended area in North Vietnam. There was so much sparkling and flashes, and shock waves.'

Satrapa enjoyed flying with a hard-charger like Teague, who would do anything for a crack at a MiG. Flying with VF-51, Teague finally got a MiG-17 in an F-4 in June 1972. Satrapa continues;

'By my 15th mission I was flying pretty good wing on "Tooter", and we did a MiGCAP around Phuc Yen – a truck park, or trans-shipment point, a non-essential target. We all knew that if we could cut the

Lt Henry Livingston goes through pre-start checks in his F-8J before launching from *Hancock* in 1972

rail lines to China, and blockade and mine Haiphong Harbour, the war would be over in six weeks. I don't know why we didn't do that (In May 1972, a large mining campaign bottled up the major port of Haiphong).

'On the MiGCAP mission there was a lot of electronic activity, so we knew there probably wouldn't be any MiGs. The A-4s dropped their bombs, and the *Iron Hands* got a couple of flak sites, and we made a couple of sweeps after they left. I noticed we were dropping down low. I looked out ahead – I was flying on "Tooter's" right side, back about 20° aft of his beam, 200 yards out. He gave me the gun signal, and I looked down and saw this airfield. I saw a MiG-17 in a revetment with people running around.

'Then I saw smoke coming over the top of "Tooter's" wing, so I knew he was shooting his cannons. I started shooting, too. I didn't know what I was hitting – I was just flying wing. We pulled up at about 550-600 knots. There was vapour coming from "Tooter's" wing.

'We egressed and I checked my watch. Once we got over water, we could light up a cigarette. That was a big deal then. We'd check each other for damage. Then I checked my map for the points of the day – "Bullseye", "Point Echo" – for geographic reference. We got back to the ship with a 500-knot break over the fantail, and trapped.

'"Hey", I said during the debrief, "as close as I could tell, that was Phuc Yen". "Tooter" looked at me and put his finger to his mouth.

'"Shhh-h!"'

Satrapa believed in outfitting himself well in case he was shot down;

'My survival gear consisted of a .357 Magnum, Model 19, with about 120 rounds, two Mk 33 grenades that I got from some buddies in an underwater demolition team at Subic Bay in the Philippines, and a 150-ft nylon line to repel out of any tree I landed in after ejecting – and a pack of cigarettes in a ziplock bag. I felt that if I ejected, I transitioned from being a fighter pilot to a foot soldier, whose main job was to get back and fly again, and to seek out and destroy the enemy.

'Many of my friends disagreed and said my only mission was to get back, avoid contact with the enemy at all costs. But I was an expert marksman, and was determined to boobytrap my parachute before heading into the jungle. I figured I could nail anyone snooping around my gear, then take their AK-47s (Soviet Kalashnikov assault rifle) and rice.

'On 19 September 1968 I was supposed to fly with "Rattler" (Lt(jg) Alex Rucker). But I had a check flight come up, and since I was the det maintenance officer, it was my job to test fly the aircraft. Tony Nargi took the TARCAP mission with "Rattler". I listened to the strike on the radio during my flight. Tony got a MiG vector, and bagged a MiG-21. "Rattler" got off a shot at the second MiG but couldn't get it. I came back with a broken glass in my attitude gyro.

'I was hit six times over Vietnam, once real bad. I was on a photo escort with an RF-8. We ingressed 60 miles north-east of Vinh. I was on his right side. That day the Vietnamese "shot from the hip". There were no electronic signals to warn us. We crossed right over the top of the site and wham! – an 85 mm shell hit me right in the tail. The hit knocked me unconscious for about three to five seconds. I woke up, and saw a karst to my right, and they hit me again. The cockpit filled with what I thought was smoke. I headed for the karst, getting ready to eject. I couldn't see my gauges and my radio wouldn't work. I reached for the dump handle on the right side to blow out the cockpit. I had tears in my eyes. I looked at the instruments and saw I had a hydraulic failure, and my generator was out. The smoke was hydraulic vapour from 3000 psi – the flak had cut that line by my foot and the vapour had filled the cockpit.

'But the engine was running smoothly, so I reversed back for the coast, toward the water. The RF-8 was with me, and I pulled out my PRC-90 and called him.

'"Hey, I'm hit, and I'm heading for the water!"

'I got over the water, and the RF-8 pilot checked me over real good and shook his head. I guess my plane looked like Swiss cheese. I relaxed and lit up a cigarette. That was the best cigarette I ever had in my life.

'I called him again, and told him to tell the ship to be ready for me. I came in to land, dirtied up from about six miles out at 8000 ft, straight in. I blew the gear down, and the wing up, except the wing wouldn't come up. They got that system too. I blew the droops, which slowed me up another 12-13 knots. They had to speed the ship up to make enough wind over the deck. After making a controllability check, I decided my minimum controllable airspeed was 150 knots – a little fast.

I trapped, hitting the barricade, with the 1-wire. There's not much room on a 27C carrier, with even the 3-wire. As soon as I hit the barricade, the damn wing came up! The aircraft (BuNo 146916) was a total strike. The target was a North Vietnamese gunnery school, and some instructor probably jumped onto the gun when we came over. Good shooting!'

Five years after his cruise with VF-194, Lt Cdr Boyd Repsher is now with VF-211 on deployment. He stands before F-8J NP 107 in full flight gear, including his red helmet with white checks of reflective tape – standard for all VF-211 pilots

EASTER INVASION 1972

Washington stopped *Rolling Thunder* missions at the end of October 1968. Although the air war entered a three-year doldrums, the fighting on the ground continued. Finally, the Communists decided to make a big push, and on the last weekend in March 1972, they thrust across the demilitarised zone, sending the South Vietnamese reeling. Most American air power had been sent home, or at least to Japan, and it was quickly rushed back to bases in South Vietnam and Thailand in order to bolster the staggering Saigon government's forces.

As the massive infusion of US air power continued, the F-8s were once

VF-211 at Miramar in 1971 before deployment. Some of the 'Checkmates' pose with Boyd Repsher's 1930 Model A Ford Roadster, fitted with a V8 engine – he still has the car. Front row, from left to right; Rick Phillips, Hank Livingston and Ben Woods. Back row, left to right; Jim Davis (CO), Boyd Repsher, Ben Hall, Phil Culson, Kevin Dwyer and Ed Brown

again back in the thick of the fighting, although they would be denied an opportunity to add to their MiG-kill list. While the RF-8s – who had never left the frontlines – flew an intensive string of reconnaissance missions, the fighters flew from the smaller-deck 27C carriers. The build-up of assets had been fast and heavy in both aircraft and men. The intensity of the war's violence had also come as a surprise.

Lt Henry Livingston was a first-tour aviator with VF-211 during this hectic phase. He joined the 'Checkmates' in April 1971 and remained with the squadron until December 1973.

On 20 June 1972 Cdr Jimmy Davis, VF-211's skipper, was shot down over Mu Gia Pass, one of three major exit routes from North Vietnam into Cambodia and Laos. He ejected from his F-8J (BuNo 150923 NP 102), which as an F-8E in 1967 had shot down a MiG-17 while being flown by VF-211's Lt Cdr Wright. Cdr Davis spent a harrowing two days and one night on the ground before he was rescued.

He strafed an area he had just bombed, violating a rule literally written in blood – never fly over the same ground twice. The 23 mm flak sounded like someone knocking on his door. His F-8's hydraulic system came up red, and the stick died. He ejected in a flat spin. When his 'chute opened, the shock was so strong it paralysed half of his body.

His squadron maintained an airborne vigil, with orbiting A-4s and an occasional F-8 working with the on-scene commander to sanitise the area. The 'Sandys' (Air Force A-1 Skyraiders from Nakhon Phanon, in Thailand) finally arrived, and Henry Livingston was on his way to the scene when one of the 'Sandy' pilots, Capt L G Highfill in A-1J serial number 52-142043, called, 'I'm hit. I'm losing it!' He bailed out, and now there were *two* pilots on the ground.

The Jolly Green Giants (Air Force rescue 'choppers') came in and got

A VF-211 F-8J refuels from a KA-3B during a CAP mission over the Gulf of Tonkin in 1972. Originally designed as a carrier-based nuclear bomber, the A-3 found its most enduring role as an airborne tanker, KA-3s literally saving hundreds of battle-damaged aircraft as they struggled back to their ships

the 'Sandy' pilot but could not retrieve Cdr Davis. The next day, a Jolly Green started his run down a valley. Davis flashed his signal mirror just as the sun went behind a cloud and the helo turned the wrong way. However, the 'driver' of the on-duty A-4 figured it out and reoriented the helo pilot. Davis caught the jungle penetrator hoist and was returned to the *Hancock* a bit too stiff to fly for a while.

Lt Livingston recalled a strange visitor soon afterward;

'Shortly after Davis' return, an Army general, bedecked with pearl-handled pistols and a big brass belt – the son of George Patton – came aboard the carrier and strode into our ready room. He demanded to know 'who the son of a bitch was' that had diverted air strikes from his military zone – III Corps in South Vietnam. We had all stood up and come to attention, but Jimmy had remained seated because of his wounds. He simply answered the irate general.

'"I did, sir!"

'The general looked at him for a moment in total silence. Then he said, "I'm damn glad to have you back, but next time, don't cost me so many air strikes". He then described what an incredible job F-8s had done bombing the town of An Loc, north of Saigon, near the Cambodian border. Surrounded by three North Vietnamese regiments, 100 mm guns and tanks, the South Vietnamese had held the town for more than 60 days, from early April to mid-June.

It was the first battle where the Communists used tanks. Every tactical Navy aircraft, including Crusaders, had been stacked up three or four flights high as they waited their turn for the forward air controllers to bring them down to bomb the town's perimeter.'

Lt Livingston had been in the An Loc operation, delivering 1000-lb bombs against enemy targets. He spotted a tank just at the time he went into a dive;

'I pulled harder, knowing I had stayed too long over the target with

During the 1971-72 cruise, Lt Cdr Repsher and Cdr Nichols (CO of VF-24) brief Capt Monger, captain of the *Hancock*

Throughout their careers, F-8s had their share of operational – non-combat – mishaps, some not of their own making. This VF-24 F-8J was in the wrong place on the flightdeck when, during an underway refuelling, one of the hoses snagged it and a nearby C-1 COD, dragging the two aircraft off the deck and onto *the oiler*. A quick-thinking chief boatswain's mate on the oiler tied the damaged aircraft down, and the smaller ship took them into the Philippines for repair!

a classic case of target fixation. Unknown to me, the North Vietnamese tank commander had abandoned his tank, and ran toward the jungle. But his crew had been chained to their positions. One bomb had fallen so close that it rattled the tank commander and he knew that another bomb would hit within 20-30 seconds. My bomb upended the tank and blew the escaping commander away.

'Gen Patton handed out two-by-three-foot blow-ups of the tank. The tank was captured and eventually set up on a cement block in Saigon as a memorial to the Battle of An Loc.'

Much to the Crusader pilots' frustration, they seldom got any MiG vectors in 1972. They firmly believed that the North Vietnamese would not engage Crusaders, waiting until the F-8s were out of the area before launching to pounce on other American aircraft, especially the Air Force F-4 fighter-bomber formations. Although the F-8s flew with the large Alpha-strike groups, they were never attacked by MiGs, yet the USAF strikers were constantly engaged by enemy fighters.

In February 1972 – a month before the Easter Invasion – two VF-211 F-8Js relieved the VF-24 BARCAP. Lt Livingston takes up the story;

'The *Chicago* (CA-13) immediately turned us south toward a "bogey" and asked us to come up on secure voice. Checking in again, we were advised that a "Red Bandit" was headed toward us from the Hanoi-Haiphong area ("Red Bandits" were MiG-17s and "Blue Bandits" were MiG-21s).

'I asked my flight lead, Ed Schrump, if he didn't smell a rat because the North Vietnamese never sent a solo -17 out over the water.

'The *Chicago* came right back with, "Oh, yeah, there are six "Blue Bandits in trail", Ed and I thought it sounded like a fair fight. Since my radar was the only "sweet one", he passed me the lead, at which point I went "under the hood", "buster", and back to our clear combat frequency – "buster" was the term for top speed to get from one point to another, and in this case the interception point.

'As our two heavy F-8s, armed with Sidewinders and cannon, blasted head-on toward the MiG gaggle, the MiG-17 began a slow left turn, effectively crossing our bow – a perfect rear-aspect intercept, except we were still 40 miles away. We were really closing, and I was out of the cockpit looking at a grey overcast with about three miles visibility. I shut down my radar at ten miles.

This F-8J of VF-24 had a landing mishap aboard the *Hancock* in 1971 off Vietnam. The deck is covered with fire-fighting foam, and the aircraft has been restrained with tie-down chains.

'Now the MiG-17 was dead ahead, but running away. At seven miles, we were still not getting good visual identification, and at five, *Chicago* ordered us to break it off because we were crossing the magic no-go line. We pressed it a few seconds more, but then began our break-away at about two-and-a-half miles, just out of 'winder range.'

During this time, Lt Cdr John Nichols, who had shot down a MiG-17 in 1968, visited the Air Force base at Udorn, Thailand, to instruct the frustrated F-4 crews in air-combat manoeuvring (ACM). USAF fighters were only breaking even against the North Vietnamese MiGs and were looking for help. Accordingly, Nichols took another VF-24 pilot, and two pilots from VF-211, along with their fighters.

The plan was to fly strikes up north with the Air Force Phantom IIs, tank, and then get in some ACM practice before recovering at Udorn. This pace kept up for several days, and each day the Navy pilots destroyed their USAF brethren, to the obvious delight of the F-8 'drivers' and the continued frustration of the air force.

USS *Bon Homme Richard* made her last Vietnam deployment in 1970, accompanied by VF-53's F-8Js. NF 203 is fully armed with four Sidewinders for its CAP mission

Nichols didn't enjoy always beating the Air Force – he was annoyed at their apparent lack of ACM training and expertise. He chastised them, none too diplomatically at times, for not using the vertical plane – the F-8's specialty – during engagements. It seemed the Air Force had completely forgotten the lessons of earlier conflicts.

Even Robin Olds – the Air Force's top MiG killer in Vietnam at the time with four victories – was angry. He heard about the Navy's visit and wangled a few rides with

As CO of VF-191, Cdr Richard A 'Pete' Peters was the first Crusader pilot to log 3000 hours in the F-8

Cdr David R 'Snake' Morris became the second 3000-hour Crusader 'driver' while skipper of VF-24. Capt A J Monger (right), skipper of the *Hancock*, helps Morris celebrate

the Udorn F-4s. Nichols recalls that after one mission and subsequent ACM session, the Phantom II with Olds in the back taxied in. The canopy barely opened when Olds' helmet flew out, followed by the irate colonel. He was furious at his pilots' poor performance.

As a parting shot, the Air Force tried to keep Nichols from flying more missions. Why? Because, he was told the grey F-8s looked too much like MiGs and were confusing the USAF pilots. He'd have to let his four Crusaders be camouflaged. At first Nichols was amenable until he asked how much weight the new paint job would add – about 1200 lbs. No way. The F-8 normally recovered with about 2000 lbs of fuel and the new paint job would cut the allowable fuel to just 800 lbs, which was totally unsatisfactory. Nichols and his detachment returned to the *Hancock*.

By 1972 the F-8 had begun disappearing from fighter squadrons. A number of units transitioned to Phantom IIs, some having made the change early enough to fly F-4s in combat in 1972. By the last full year of the war, only four fighter squadrons flew the F-8 – VF-24 and VF-211 in the *Hancock*, and VF-191 and VF-194 in the *Oriskany*. All four squadrons flew the F-8J. Of course, VFP-63's detachments continued to fly the RF-8G.

The 27C carriers had largely retired by this time, too, which limited the deck space available to the Crusader. With older ships like *Ticonderoga*, *Intrepid*, *Shangri-la* and *Bon Homme Richard* gone, only *Hancock* and *Oriskany* remained in the frontline.

In keeping with its long period of service, and sterling combat record, the Crusader eventually boasted five pilots who attained over 3000 hours in various models of the F-8. The first man to gain the magic number of hours was Cdr Richard A 'Pete' Peters, who flew his 3000th hour in the F-8 in November 1971. Peters also accumulated nearly 800 carrier landings in the F-8, more than any other Crusader pilot. Cdr (later Rear Adm) David R Morris followed in July 1972. MiG killer Commander John B Nichols III flew his 3000th hour in August 1973, whilst Lt Cdr (later Vice Adm) Jerry Unruh got there in September 1974. Cdr (later Rear Adm) W F Flagg became the fifth, and last, 3000-hour Crusader 'driver' in 1978, and with 3272 hours, he also garnered the 'high-time' slot of all F-8 pilots.

Now-Cdr Nichols, CO of VF-24, listens to a brief in his squadron's ready room aboard the *Hancock* during the 1972-73 cruise

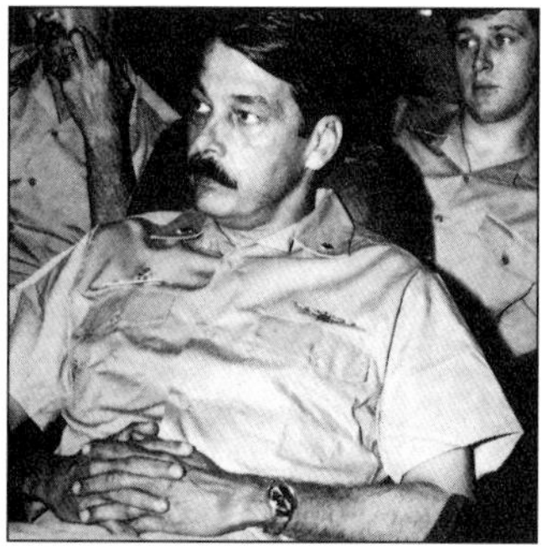

The *Hancock* returns from another combat cruise, her crew members spelling out their sentiments after months away

The Crusader's last months in Vietnam are filled with amazing stories, but none is more incredible than that involving Cdr John Nichols' VF-24 in the *Hancock* in 1973. While the cease-fire of in January of that year had ended the fighting, the old carrier continued roving the South China Sea, *Hancock* conducting normal operations in the Gulf of Tonkin throughout the summer and early fall of 1973. But she received orders in late October to go south toward the Indian Ocean, then to the Arabian Sea. She began the transit on 29 October and arrived at the southern end of the Red Sea as the third Arab-Israeli War was winding down.

The squadron commanding officers of Air Wing 21 listened in amazement as they were told to stand by to fly their A-4s and F-8s to Israel and turn them over to the hard-pressed Israel Air Force. CVW-21 included three A-4 squadrons – VA-55, VA-164 and VA-212 – and the two veteran F-8 squadrons, VF-24 and VF-211. A-4s were coming from the United States, through transoceanic flights, including stops on carriers in

Shortly after returning from their 1975-76 cruise, the F-8Js of VF-194 did FCLPs at NAS Miramar, although they would never again deploy. Here, a 'Red Lightning' Crusader passes the LSO monitoring the practice carrier approach (*Peter Mersky*)

the Mediterranean. But the plan to completely turn over an air wing's assets to the Israelis upset many CVW-21 pilots.

They began to ask questions. 'Will we be armed during the flight? Can we shoot back at the Arabs? What'll we do after we arrive?' The briefers did not, or could not, answer these questions satisfactorily, and the air in the ready rooms was tense. However, the Israelis had gained the upper hand in the war, and the *Hancock* was sent on its way back to the United States.

F-8Js of VF-191 during their last deployment in late 1975 in the *Oriskany*. It was the old carrier's last trip as well (*via Chuck Scott*)

A view of *Oriskany* on her last deployment. A VF-191 F-8J is on the No 1 catapult as the ship's H-2 plane guard slowly paces the old carrier

'LEATHERNECK' CRUSADERS, 1965-68

Along with Navy squadrons, five Marine Corps F-8 units saw a great deal of combat in Vietnam. As previously described, VMF(AW)-212 was *Oriskany*'s second fighter squadron during CVW-16's 1965 cruise, the 'Lancers'' CO, Lt Col Charles Ludden, taking over the wing when Cdr James Stockdale was shot down in September. It was the first time since World War 2 that a Marine had commanded a carrier air wing, and the last time a Marine squadron flew from a carrier as part of the embarked air wing until 1971.

However, most of the Marines' activity came from shore-based squadrons. In Vietnam, the fixed-wing jet squadrons operated mainly from two bases, Da Nang and the smaller, but important, base at Chu Lai, 55 miles south of Da Nang.

As the influx of squadrons continued throughout 1965, VMF(AW)-312 Checkerboards' brought its F-8Es to Da Nang on 19 December as part of Marine Aircraft Group (MAG) 11 under Col Robert F Conley, an experienced aviator who, as a member of VMF(N)-513 flying F3D Skynights in Korea, had downed a MiG-15 at night in January 1953 – his son was killed in action flying Phantom IIs with VMFA-115 in September 1968.

The 'Checkerboards' had fought to come to Vietnam after they learned they would be rotated back to the 'States. Lt Col R B Newport and his men demanded a chance to join their fellow Marines, and had eventually flown 718 combat missions by February 1966.

When VMF(AW)-312 returned home to transition to F-4s, it left its F-8Es in Vietnam for its replacement unit, VMF(AW)-235, led by Lt Col George A Gibson. The 'Death Angels', whose squadron motto was *Ride Nunc* (Laugh Now)

MAG-11 commander Col Robert Conley (left) confers with Lt Col Dick Newport, CO of VMF(AW)-312, at Atsugi in 1964

Col Conley stands beside his appropriately decorated Studebaker sedan and an F-8E of VMF(AW)-312 at NAS Atsugi. Squadron CO, Lt Col Dick Newport, is in the Crusader's cockpit

quickly became the most recognised of Marine Crusader squadrons during the war, sporting bright red noses with white stars. Arriving at Da Nang on 1 February 1966, -235 quickly got into the action.

During this early stage of the conflict, not all the fighting was between the Americans and the Communists. The South Vietnamese, unused to taking orders from their American allies, occasionally resisted. A rebellion in April 1965 by a small faction in the South Vietnamese Army precipitated a confrontation between the 9th Marine Regiment and a well-armed South Vietnamese force at a bridge.

The arrogant South Vietnamese commander threatened he would use his 155 mm howitzers against the Marines. Undaunted, the American Marine CO, Col John R Chaisson, glanced up just as a flight of VMF(AW)-235 Crusaders, armed with bombs and rockets, roared overhead. Looking the Vietnamese commander in the eye, he growled, 'I'll see those 155s and raise you two F-8s'. The South Vietnamese backed down.

VMF(AW)-235 was relieved by VMF(AW)-232, under Lt Col N M Trapnell, Jr, on 15 November 1966. The 'Red Devils' took over -235's veteran F-8Es and began flying combat missions in December. Their 2000-lb bombs were very effective against enemy concentrations in the dense jungles of the area.

VMF(AW)-232 suffered its first combat loss on 4 May 1967, although the pilot involved, Maj E F Townley flying F-8E BuNo 150316, was res-

An F-8E of VMF(AW)-232 taxies at Da Nang in 1967 (*NMNA*)

Two 'Red Devil' pilots prepare to take the runway for a mission in April 1967. Note the widely differing bombloads of the two F-8s – a probable indication of the chronic shortage of bombs at this time

cued. Capt H J Hellbach was not as fortunate after he radioed he had taken flak hits during a mission 15 days later, his Crusader (BuNo 149213) exploding before he could eject. The 'Red Devils' left South Vietnam on 30 June 1967, having flown 5785 sorties.

The 'Death Angels' of VMF(AW)-235 – the most active of the three in-country Marine fighter squadrons – subsequently returned to the action, and in May 1967 flew a record 854 sorties in support of Marine Corps ground forces. The squadron eventually completed 9140 day and night combat missions over North and South Vietnam.

Then-Capt David C Corbett remembers -235 as 'the wildest bunch of crazies I have had the pleasure to serve with . . . that last bunch of "drivers" were kicked out of practically every O Club in the Orient during 1967-68, but how they could fly the F-8'. Corbett also fondly remembers his time in the Crusader. 'I would have been happy to fly an entire career in the F-8 – it was a pilot's aircraft'. Corbett later joined HMA-369 to fly AH-1J Seacobras in 1972 as part of the Marine Hunter-Killer (MARHUK) operation against Communist river traffic.

During the February 1968 Seige of Khe Sanh, VMF(AW)-235 flew in support of Operation *Niagara* – the massive air operation that included Navy, Marine and Air Force aircraft in a continuous attack against communist positions. Now-Col Corbett recalls that period;

'Tet '68 had just started, and to read the papers, we were losing our butts. In reality, the Marines in I Corps "kicked tail", not the least of that action took place at Khe Sanh. The F-8 was the only aircraft that could carry the monster 2000-pounders, and we cleared a lot of helo landing zones.

'During a period of about three weeks, we worked very closely with the "grunts" defending Khe Sanh. They were in a bad way because it was difficult to re-supply them. The bad guys were attacking them in every possible way. The most effective method was to tunnel toward the perimeter wire, pop up, and attack the Marine positions. This had to be stopped. Someone decided to use our F-8s.

'We flew mission after mission, dropping our big bombs only about 300 ft from our own positions – the closest we'd ever tried. The bombs had delayed fuses which allowed them to penetrate two or three feet into the ground before they exploded. When they went off, whole sections of the tunnels would collapse. The plan worked better than we expected and the enemy's drive to take Khe Sanh was squashed. I can't imagine how the grunts felt about us dropping so close, but they apparently had a lot of confidence in us, and it paid off.'

Dave Corbett had a lot of experience with the huge Mk 84s. Although he complained that the F-8's bomb sight was not very good – he recalled that he and other pilots used a simple grease-pencil mark on their sights which, when properly aligned in conjunction with the individual pilot's most comfortable seat position, gave fairly consistent results;

'When four Crusaders were each loaded with two Mk 84s fused with 36-inch "Daisy Cutters", the devastation to the landscape was incredible to say the least. On one mission, I remember that with a total of eight 2000-pounders, we completely levelled an entire mountain. I was so impressed that I actually went down low and slow to see the results. It was terrible, but very effective.

'Another time, I dropped these same weapons on troops in the open. The enemy was literally cut in half. The "Daisy Cutter" exploded 36 inches above the ground, and in my opinion, against troops in the open and for clearing landing zones, there was no more effective weapon.'

Peter D Williams, a retired major general, was a captain with VMF(AW)-235 in 1967. He had flown Crusaders in VMF(AW)-212, although not during the 'Lancers'' *Oriskany* deployment, and appreciated the F-8E;

'The Crusader had a big cockpit – very roomy. The pilot sat way out in front of the nosegear, which made for some anxious moments on carriers when plane captains taxied you out over the deck edge – or so it seemed.

'The 'burner had a very hard light . . . Boom! It was easy to identify an F-8 taking off just by the sound.'

When Williams, who went by the name of 'Drax', joined the squadron in August, he could see the F-8s were war-weary. The pilots were limited to 1.2 mach, and every aircraft wore patches, especially along the leading edges of the unit horizontal tail (UHT).

'Some birds required a maintenance brief before flight', he related. There were also certain precautions a pilot had to take. "When it was damp and humid – like in the monsoon season – our gloves would be wet with sweat. Some planes gave us mild shocks through the landing gear handle when we raised or lowered the gear. The solution was slipping a condom over the handle.

Capt 'Drax' Williams leans on a 2000-lb 'fat' bomb before a mission in a VMF(AW)-235 F-8E in August 1967

'The F-8 was a pilot's aeroplane. You felt you were sitting on the nose of a rocket, with almost 60 ft of engine, wings and tail behind you. I never tired of looking at the aircraft. It remains to this day for me the most graceful aircraft I've ever seen in flight. On the ground with its wing raised, it looked powerful and menacing.

'Although sometimes hard to land, especially aboard ship, it flew like a dream, and at altitude it was unbeatable. It let you know when you were approaching the edge of the envelope and departed flight spectacularly if you didn't listen.

'The F-8 was a great aeroplane for strafing. You could hit anything you could see. Four streams of bullets would converge 3000 ft ahead of you, and you could literally put 400 rounds through a doorway. Trucks, buildings, light armour, and most unhardened point targets didn't stand a chance.'

Another -235 aviator was then-Capt Orson Swindle, who made the 1966 deployment to Da Nang. After flying 185 missions, he was transferred to the staff of 1 MAW, but he still maintained his currency with the 'Red Noses'. However, on his 205th mission, on 11 November 1966, his F-8E (BuNo 150858) was downed over North Vietnam, and he began six years as a PoW. Ejecting at a 60° angle as the ground rushed up at him, as he hung in his 'chute he saw several North Vietnamese shooting at him.

Swindle subsequently endured beatings and torture at the hands of the Communists, before being taken to the main prison in Hanoi, the infamous 'Hanoi Hilton'. Finally released on 4 March 1973, he was repatriated, resumed his flying duties, and eventually retired as a lieutenant colonel in 1979. His experience was typical of many of the aviator-prisoners held by the North Vietnamese.

Denis J Kiely was another young captain who flew with VMF(AW)-235. However, he had already seen considerable combat as a photo-pilot with a shipboard detachment of VMCJ-1 on board *Kitty Hawk* – his experiences in RF-8As are described in the companion volume.

Reporting to -235 in September 1967 as a recently selected major, Kiely found himself in a unit that was top-heavy with rank – there were 15 majors in the squadron of 21 pilots. He regularly flew with 'Drax' Williams and Gary Post.

Like other 'drivers' in the squadron, Kiely dropped his share of heavy bombs, including Mk 84s and Mk 65s. He vividly remembers a mission during the 1968 Tet Offensive, which was one of the most intense periods of combat the Marines faced during the war;

'On 24 February Capt Post and I scrambled to support Marines at Hue City. The weather was awful, really below minimums on take-off, with solid clouds to 20,000 ft. The weather over the target wasn't much better, the best conditions promising a ceiling below 300 ft.

'As Gary and I descended to make our runs, we broke out at 200 ft. The FAC in a Marine O-1 had been shot down and killed, but we wanted to try anyway because the "grunts" hadn't been able to get air support for days because of the weather, and it was hard trying to blast the NVA (North Vietnamese Army) out of the Citadel.

The "Ice Man" (Capt Post) and I set up our runs as some brave lad on the ground fired a 3.5-inch rocket at a tower (the Dong Ba tower) where the NVA had set up a heavy machine gun. I could see the gunner shooting at me as I fired my cannons. I hit the tower, then shot off a Zuni, which went right through the tower and blew with a roar *I heard*.

'As Post made his run, he seemed to be at or below the Citadel wall! At the last instant, he popped over the wall, dropped lower, and virtually hand-delivered two "nape cans" into the laps of the NVA! All of this in rain, below 300 ft and at 450 knots.'

This important NVA position was finally taken by a concerted ground effort by the 5th Marines.

A month after that mission, Maj Kiely and Capt Post again came to the aid of the Marines on the ground. On 16 March they dropped napalm on North Vietnamese troops, followed by several strafing passes. All the

Maj Kiely in a Crusader that boasts mission bomb markings. The pilot used the strap behind him to pull down the canopy

while, their Crusaders took hits from small arms fire Post's aircraft (BuNo 149225) rapidly beginning to lose fuel. They headed for the safety of the water, where Post eventually ejected and was rescued. Maj Kiely remembered, 'Later, I met the men of the company we had helped. When someone told them I had been the flight leader of the F-8s that day, many of them came over to shake my hand and say thanks. It was a moment I'll always savour.'

Squadron CO Lt Col Wallace N Wessel goes through systems checks with his plane captain, who is 'dressed' for South Vietnam's climate. Note the 'fat' 2000-lb bomb and full load of Zuni tubes on the Crusader

Commenting on the F-8's ability to absorb battle damage, Maj Kiely says;

'Much has been said of the Crusader's vulnerability. I can attest to the opposite. I took hits from 12.7 mm, 14.5 mm, 37 mm and 57 mm fire – on one occasion several hits from 14.5 mm and 37 mm nearly blew the guns out of the port side of my plane. My wingman told me I was on fire, trailing a lot of flame and smoke.

'I had one shrapnel hole in the cockpit, and my fire-warning light was on steady. My number two was hollering at me to eject when I saw I was still in 'burner. As I pulled the throttle back to military, he said the smoke went from black to grey. I saw the firing warning light dim. I swallowed hard and headed for the sea.

'Despite a lot of airframe damage, the loss of two hydraulic systems, and other problems, the old 'Gator motored home, the air bottles functioning perfectly for me to raise the wing and lower the gear.

'When we looked the plane over, we found that one heavy calibre shell had hit the belly just aft of the turbine of the J-57 (engine), ripping out the spray bars for the afterburner, then passing through the upper fuselage before detonating. Raw fuel spewing from the ruptured fuel line caused the fire. Once I had secured the afterburner, the flames went out.

Besides the four Marine squadrons that flew F-8s in South-East Asia, a fifth squadron, VMCJ-1, flew the RF-8A. One of three Marine composite squadrons, VMCJ-1, also operated the Korean War-vintage Douglas EF-10B Skyknight. Both aircraft performed yeoman service throughout the 1964-68 period of the war – VMCJ-1's service is described in the companion volume on RF-8s.

Toting as many bombs as will be seen on an F-8, as well as a full load of Zunis, these two VMF(AW)-235 aircraft begin their lengthy take-off roll from Da Nang

THE FINAL WORD

Most, if not all, Crusader pilots loved their F-8s – with certain reservations, mainly regarding flying around the ship. Here is a sampling of how various men in this narrative felt about the F-8, and the unpopular and ultimately unsuccessful war they fought with her. Again, Bud Flagg;

'At the end of the first cruise, every time we went across the beach I'd get very nervous and break out into a cold sweat. Once we crossed the beach, and got involved in the heat of battle, we did what we were supposed to do, but we constantly asked ourselves who was going to get hit, or come back.

'Every strike we flew, we lost at least one plane, sometimes the pilot. It was an eerie feeling at the briefs. Both A-4 squadrons, especially, took heavy casualties in planes and pilots. Our Marines lost four planes – two in combat – and one pilot.

'The second cruise, in 1966, VF-162 went through 12 F-8s and five pilots. That was within three-and-a-half months, since that was the cruise which was cut short by the *Oriskany*'s fire in October. The losses were not all in combat, some were operational – ramp strike, bridle "slaps" – as well as flak and SAM losses. Four were actual combat losses.

'I think it was a war everyone would like to forget. All the young guys, myself included, thought it was something we had to get into, wear medals, the glory side, never realising what a major part this would be of our lives, the stress and strain we were under, and how, in later years, this stress would surface. When you've been scared out of your wits, I'm not sure you ever fully recover from it. When they began using missiles, that was another type of sheer terror. You knew you could avoid the missiles, but to see these huge things coming at you was awesome, and your heart stood still. It was hard, sometimes, to even call out the missile. I think

Maj Kiely by the squadron 'tori' signpost at Da Nang in 1967

the Vietnamese sometimes just "lobbed" the SAMs at us to see if they could hit anything.

Marine aviator retired-Colonel 'Deej' Kiely;

'On the ground, she was a sight to behold, a daunting mix of grace, beauty and blemishes. Approaching her on the line was like catching a fashion model without her make-up. Long and slender, the Crusader sat on close-tracked landing gear that appeared ready to collapse under the weight of her 58-ft frame, and the ramp beneath her was slick with leaking hydraulic fluid. Flaps, droops, and her huge speedbrake generally hung at odd angles.

'The "nugget" on his FAM-1 approached the F-8 with anticipation and foreboding; this was not just any plane. As you got to know her, felt the rush of power from 18,000 lbs of thrust, fired her guns and out-manoeuvred anything in the sky, your affection for this beautiful fighter took on the aura of a religious experience.'

Dick Wyman also appreciated the Crusader;

'It was definitely one of the highs of my life to fly the F-8. It was my super sports car, my raging stallion, and I loved to fly it to the edge and make it dance for me.

'Yet, I always respected the Crusader, and knew if I got careless it would get me. I got shot up, hit power lines, launched with zero fuel and landed with a damaged nose gear that did not come down. It was the most exciting aircraft I ever flew.'

Bob Kirkwood did have concerns;

'The F-8 was wonderful to fly when cleaned up and moving. In the landing configuration, though, gear and flaps down, there were problems – more of an idiosyncrasy, a subtle tendency. Something in the variable-incidence wing weakened the connection between the throttle and the descent rate, maybe the nose position and airspeed, too. Pilots compensated by working harder without realising it.

'During the day, we came ripping into the break in perfect echelon, usually faster than the course rules allowed. We broke with exaggerated precision and made perfect landings. We denied there was anything the F-8 couldn't handle. But at night, when all the peripheral cues disappeared, a lot of the fun also disappeared.

'The F-8 was not a completely honest aeroplane when dirty, not like the Grumman TF-9J, which I flew as an instrument instructor in the early 1960s. The Cougar could be stabilised on glideslope and kept there with tiny throttle adjustments.

'Clean, the F-8 was quick and nimble, a joy to fly.'

The men of the F-8 squadrons remain some of the most colourful characters and accomplished aviators in the history of naval aviation. Their only equals are the men of the reconnaissance squadrons and the RF-8A and RF-8G photo-Crusaders, many of whom 'cross-pollinated' from one community to the other. In a profession that requires such a high level of skill and dedication, the F-8 demanded – and received – a step above that standard.

In these days of computer-driven, HUD-and-glass-cockpit-equipped, multi-mission, multi-crew tactical jets, it is doubtful that we shall see the likes of Vought's sleek, sexy, Crusader, and its special breed of 'driver', again.

APPENDICES

APPENDIX A

GLOSSARY

AAA - Antiaircraft Artillery

Alpha Strike – A large offensive air strike, involving all the carrier air wing's assets, fighters, attack, refuelling, etc

BARCAP – Barrier Combat Air Patrol. A fighter patrol between the carrier task force and enemy threat

CAG – Commander Air Group. A somewhat archaic term, as wing designation was changed to CVW, and the commander was subsequently referred to as CAW, but CAG remained part of the vocabulary

CAP – Combat Air Patrol

CV – Aircraft carrier. During Vietnam, normal acronym was CVA, designating an *attack* carrier, where CVS indicated an *anti-submarine* carrier. In 1975 the Navy dispensed with CVA and CVS, using CV to indicate the integrated role of the carrier

CVW – Carrier Air Wing

LSO – Landing Signal Officer

MiGCAP – Standing patrol over the fleet or strike force to protect against any threat from enemy aircraft

OINC – Officer-in-Charge

SAM – Surface-to-Air Missile. A generic term, but usually referring to the Soviet-built SA-2 Guideline

SAR – Search and Rescue

TARCAP – Target Combat Air Patrol. Fighters tasked with providing escort protection for the strike force

Trap – An arrested landing aboard a carrier

VA – Navy Light Attack Squadron

VF – Navy Fighter Squadron

VFP – Navy Light Photographic Squadron

VMCJ – Marine Composite Reconnaissance Squadron

VMF – Marine Fighter Squadron. (AW) was added in 1967 to denote all-weather capability, but was a short-lived designation and was overtaken by VMFA, for fighter and attack

APPENDIX B

F-8 MIG-KILLERS

Pilot	Squadron	Date	Model	BuNo Modex	Type MiG
Cdr Hal Marr	VF-211	12 June 1966	F-8E	150924* NP 103	MiG-17**
Lt(jg) Phil Vampatella	VF-211	21 June 1966	F-8E	150300* NP 104	MiG-17
Lt Eugene Chancy	VF-211	21 June 1966	F-8E	150910# NP 101(?)	MiG-17
Cdr Dick Bellinger	VF-162	9 October 1966	F-8E	149159 AH 210	MiG-21
Lt Cdr M O Wright	VF-211	1 May 1967	F-8E	150923* NP 110	MiG-17
Cdr Paul Speer	VF-211	19 May 1967	F-8E	150348 NP 101(?)	MiG-17
Lt(jg) Joseph Shea	VF-211	19 May 1967	F-8E	150661 NP 102(?)	MiG-17
Lt Cdr Bobby Lee	VF-24	19 May 1967	F-8C	146981 NP 44?	MiG-17
Lt Phil Wood	VF-24	19 May 1967	F-8C	147029+ NP 443	MiG-17
Cdr Marion Isaacks	VF-24	21 July 1967	F-8C	147018 NP 442	MiG-17
Lt Cdr Robert Kirkwood	VF-24	21 July 1967	F-8C	146992 NP 447	MiG-17
Lt Cdr Tim Hubbard	VF-211	21 July 1967	F-8E	150859# NP 107	MiG-17
Lt Richard Wyman	VF-162	14 December 1967	F-8E	150879 AH 204	MiG-17
Lt Cdr L R Myers	VF-51	26 June 1968	F-8H	148710 NL 116	MiG-21
Lt Cdr John Nichols	VF-191	9 July 1968	F-8E	150926# NM 101	MiG-17
Lt Cdr Guy Cane	VF-53	29 July 1968	F-8E	150349 NF 203	MiG-17
Lt Norm McCoy	VF-51	1 August 1968	F-8H	147916 NF 102	MiG-21
Lt Tony Nargi	VF-111	9 September 1968	F-8C	146961 AK 103	MiG-21
Lt Jerry Tucker	VF-211	23 May 1972	F-8J	150900 NP 101	MiG-17++

Key
***** Subsequently lost to enemy flak
+ Struck because of heavy battle damage
# Subsequently lost to operational causes
++ Not officially credited because MiG pilot ejected before Lieutenant Tucker could fire
****** Cdr Marr hit a second MiG-17, which was subsequently confirmed but never officially credited – see chapter six
(?) There is no information available, even from the pilot, that confirms the F-8's side number

APPENDIX C

F-8 SQUADRON DEPLOYMENTS IN VIETNAM

Squadron/Air Wing	Model	Carrier	Tail Code and Modex	Dates
VF-24 'Checkertails'				
VF-24/CVW-21	F-8C	*Hancock*	NP 4xx	21 Oct 64 to 29 May 65
VF-24/CVW-21	F-8C	*Hancock*	NP 4xx	10 Nov 65 to 1 Aug 66
VF-24/CVW-21	F-8C	*Bon Homme Richard*	NP 4xx	26 Jan 67 to 25 Aug 67
VF-24/CVW-21	F-8H	*Hancock*	NP 2xx	18 Jul 68 to 3 Mar 69
VF-24/CVW-21	F-8H	*Hancock*	NP 2xx	2 Aug 69 to 15 Apr 70
VF-24/CVW-21	F-8J	*Hancock*	NP 2xx	22 Oct 70 to 2 Jun 71
VF-24/CVW-21	F-8J	*Hancock*	NP 2xx	7 Jan 72 to 3 Oct 72
VF-24/CVW-21	F-8J	*Hancock*	NP 2xx	8 May 73 to 8 Jan 74
VF-24/CVW-21	F-8J	*Hancock*	NP 2xx	18 Mar 75 to 20 Oct 75
VF-51 'Screaming Eagles'				
VF-51/CVW-5	F-8E	*Ticonderoga*	NF 1xx	3 Jan 63 to 15 Jul 63
VF-51/CVW-5	F-8E	*Ticonderoga*	NF 1xx	14 Apr 64 to 15 Dec 64
VF-51/CVW-5	F-8E	*Ticonderoga*	NF 1xx	28 Sep 65 to 13 May 66
VF-51/CVW-5	F-8E	*Hancock*	NF 1xx	5 Jan 67 to 22 Jul 67
VF-51/CVW-5	F-8H	*Bon Homme Richard*	NF 1xx	27 Jan 68 to 10 Oct 68
VF-51/CVW-5	F-8J	*Bon Homme Richard*	NF 1xx	18 Mar 69 to 29 Oct 69
VF-51/CVW-5	F-8J	*Bon Homme Richard*	NF 1xx	2 Apr 70 to 12 Nov 70
VF-53 'Iron Angels'				
VF-53/CVW-5	F-8E	*Ticonderoga*	NF 2xx	3 Jan 63 to 15 Jul 63
VF-53/CVW-5	F-8E	*Ticonderoga*	NF 2xx	14 Apr 64 to 15 Dec 64
VF-53/CVW-5	F-8E	*Ticonderoga*	NF 2xx	28 Sep 65 to 13 May 66
VF-53/CVW-5	F-8E	*Hancock*	NF 2xx	5 Jan 67 to 22 Jul 67
VF-53/CVW-5	F-8E	*Bon Homme Richard*	NF 2xx	27 Jan 68 to 10 Oct 68
VF-53/CVW-5	F-8J	*Bon Homme Richard*	NF 2xx	18 Mar 69 to 29 Oct 69
VF-53/CVW-5	F-8J	*Bon Homme Richard*	NF 2xx	2 Apr 70 to 12 Nov 70
VF-111 'Sundowners'				
VF-111/CVW-11	F-8D	*Kitty Hawk*	NH 1xx	17 Oct 63 to 20 Jul 64
VF-111/CVW-2	F-8D	*Midway*	NE 4xx	6 Mar 65 to 23 Nov 65
VF-111/CVW-16	F-8E	*Oriskany*	AH 1xx	26 May 66 to 16 Nov 66
VF-111/Det 11/CVW-10	F-8C	*Intrepid*	AH 1xx	11 May 67 to 30 Dec 67
VF-111/CVW-16	F-8C	*Oriskany*	AH 1xx	16 Jun 67 to 31 Jan 68
VF-111/Det 11/CVW-10	F-8C	*Intrepid*	AK 1xx	4 Jun 68 to 8 Feb 69
VF-111/CVW-16	F-8H	*Ticonderoga*	AH 1xx	1 Feb 69 to 18 Sep 69
VF-111/CVW-8	F-8H	*Shangri-la*	AJ 1xx	5 Mar 70 to 17 Dec 70
VF-154 'Black Knights'				
VF-154/CVW-15	F-8D	*Coral Sea*	NL 4xx	7 Dec 64 to 1 Nov 65
VF-162 'Hunters'				
VF-162/CVW-16	F-8E	*Oriskany*	AH 2xx	5 Apr 65 to 16 Dec 65
VF-162/CVW-16	F-8E	*Oriskany*	AH 2xx	26 May 66 to 16 Nov 66
VF-162/CVW-16	F-8E	*Oriskany*	AH 2xx	16 Jun 67 to 31 Jan 68
VF-162/CVW-16	F-8J	*Ticonderoga*	AH 2xx	1 Feb 69 to 18 Sep 69
VF-162/CVW-8	F-8H	*Shangri-la*	AJ 2xx	5 Mar 70 to 17 Dec 70
VF-191 'Satan's Kittens'				
VF-191/CVW-19	F-8E	*Bon Homme Richard*	NM 1xx	28 Jan 64 to 21 Nov 64
VF-191/CVW-19	F-8E	*Bon Homme Richard*	NM 1xx	21 Apr 65-13 Jan 66
VF-191/CVW-19	F-8E	*Ticonderoga*	NM 1xx	15 Oct 66 to 29 May 67
VF-191/CVW-19	F-8E	*Ticonderoga*	NM 1xx	27 Dec 67 to 17 Aug 68

VF-191/CVW-19	F-8J	*Oriskany*	NM 1xx	16 Apr 69 to 17 Nov 69
VF-191/CVW-19	F-8J	*Oriskany*	NM 1xx	14 May 70 to 10 Dec 70
VF-191/CVW-19	F-8J	*Oriskany*	NM 1xx	14 May 71 to 18 Dec 71
VF-191/CVW-19	F-8J	*Oriskany*	NM 1xx	5 Jun 72 to 30 Mar 73
VF-191/CVW-19	F-8J	*Oriskany*	NM 1xx	18 Oct 73 to 5 Jun 74
VF-191/CVW-19	F-8J	*Oriskany*	NM 1xx	16 Sep 75 to 3 Mar 76

VF-194 'Red Lightnings'

VF-194/CVW-19	F-8C	*Bon Homme Richard*	NM 4xx	28 Jan 64 to 21 Nov 64
VF-194/CVW-19	F-8E	*Bon Homme Richard*	NM 4xx	21 Apr 65 to 13 Jan 66
VF-194/CVW-19	F-8E	*Ticonderoga*	NM 4xx	15 Oct 66 to 29 May 67
VF-194/CVW-19	F-8E	*Ticonderoga*	NM 4xx	27 Dec 67 to 17 Aug 68
VF-194/CVW-19	F-8J	*Oriskany*	NM 2xx	16 Apr 69 to 17 Nov 69
VF-194/CVW-19	F-8J	*Oriskany*	NM 2xx	14 May 70 to 10 Dec 70
VF-194/CVW-19	F-8J	*Oriskany*	NM 2xx	14 May 71 to 18 Dec 71
VF-194/CVW-19	F-8J	*Oriskany*	NM 2xx	5 Jun 72 to 30 Mar 73
VF-194/CVW-19	F-8J	*Oriskany*	NM 2xx	18 Oct 73 to 5 Jun 74
VF-194/CVW-19	F-8J	*Oriskany*	NM 2xx	16 Sep 75 to 3 Mar 76

VF-211 'Checkmates'

VF-211/CVW-21	F-8E	*Hancock*	NP 1xx	21 Oct 64 to 29 May 65
VF-211/CVW-21	F-8E	*Hancock*	NP 1xx	10 Nov 65 to 1 Aug 66
VF-211/CVW-21	F-8E	*Bon Homme Richard*	NP 1xx	26 Jan 67 to 25 Aug 67
VF-211/CVW-21	F-8H	*Hancock*	NP 1xx	18 Jul 68 to 3 Mar 69
VF-211/CVW-21	F-8H	*Hancock*	NP 1xx	2 Aug 69 to 15 Apr 70
VF-211/CVW-21	F-8J	*Hancock*	NP 1xx	22 Oct 70 to 2 Jun 71
VF-211/CVW-21	F-8J	*Hancock*	NP 1xx	7 Jan 72 to 3 Oct 72
VF-211/CVW-21	F-8J	*Hancock*	NP 1xx	8 May 73 to 8 Jan 74
VF-211/CVW-21	F-8J	*Hancock*	NP 1xx	18 Mar 75 to 20 Oct 75

VMF(AW)-212 'Lancers'

VMF(AW)-212/CVW-16	F-8E	*Oriskany*	WD 1xx	5 Apr 65 to 16 Dec 65

VMF(AW)-312 'Checkerboards'

VMF(AW)-312	F-8E	Da Nang, RVn	DR 1x	Dec 65 to Feb 66

VMF(AW)-232 'Red Devils'

VMF(AW)-232	F-8E	Da Nang, RVn	WT 1x	Nov 66 to Sep 67

VMF(AW)-235 'Death Angels'

VMF(AW)-235	F-8E	Da Nang, RVn	DB 1x	Feb 66 to Nov 66
				Feb 67 to May 68

Note: The four Marine Corps F-8 squadrons that served in Vietnam all transitioned to the F-4B or F-4J Phantom IIs and redesignated as VMFAs. Only two of these squadrons, VMFA-212 and VMFA-232, took their Phantom IIs to Vietnam in 1972. VMFA-212 served a shortened tour before returning to Hawaii, while VMFA-232 flew alongside VMFA-115 through to the middle of 1973, participating in the last US missions in South-East Asia.

APPENDIX D

SUMMING UP FOR THE RECORD

A bean count is always hazardous. Records are fluid things, and data can be changed or refined. However, here is one version of how the F-8 fared in combat in South-East Asia.

The Navy lost ten fighters to SAMs and 42 to flak and small arms (hand-held weapons). Sixty-six Navy F-8s were lost in operational mishaps. Twenty Navy RF-8s were lost to flak, whilst no Marine Corps RF-8s were lost. Thus, including three confirmed losses to MiGs in 1966, and one possible in 1972 (VF-211 F-8J BuNo 150311, downed on 24 May 1972 – pilot, Lt C R Beeler made a PoW), the Navy lost 56 F-8s and 20 RF-8s in combat. Fifty-eight fighters and nine 'photo-birds' were lost to operational causes. Of these, the greatest amount lost of a single model – the F-8E – was 42 (30 Navy and 12 Marine Corps). Overall, 12 per cent of all Crusaders manufactured were lost in South-East Asia.

The Navy squadron that lost the most Crusaders in combat was VF-111 with 12, including one to a MiG. VF-162 followed with ten, with one lost to a MiG, whilst VF-211 lost eight F-8s (again, including at least one, maybe two, to MiGs). VF-191 and VF-194 each lost five, VF-24 lost seven and VF-154 six.

The Marine Corps squadrons at Da Nang kept their F-8Es at the base, merely rotating them around. Thus, it should not be surprising that many of the war-weary Crusaders' individual luck eventually ran out. VMF(AW)-235 led the loss column with seven, while VMF(AW)-232 tallied three combat losses.

The Marines lost 12 F-8Es to flak and SAMS in South-East Asia, plus two during enemy rocket attacks on bases. Fifteen Crusaders were operational losses – non-combat-related problems like system malfunction, weather, and pilot error.

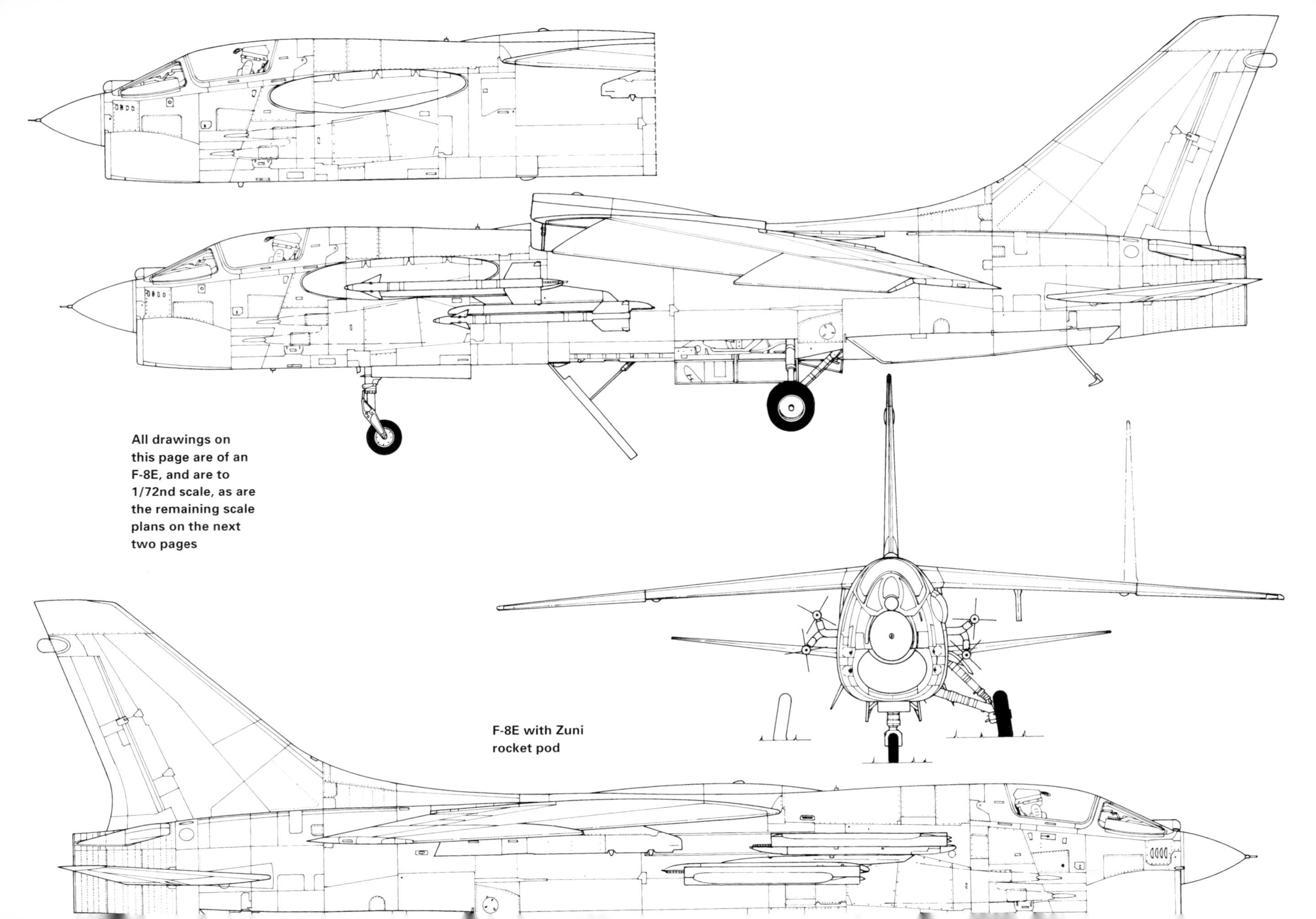

All drawings on this page are of an F-8E, and are to 1/72nd scale, as are the remaining scale plans on the next two pages

F-8E with Zuni rocket pod

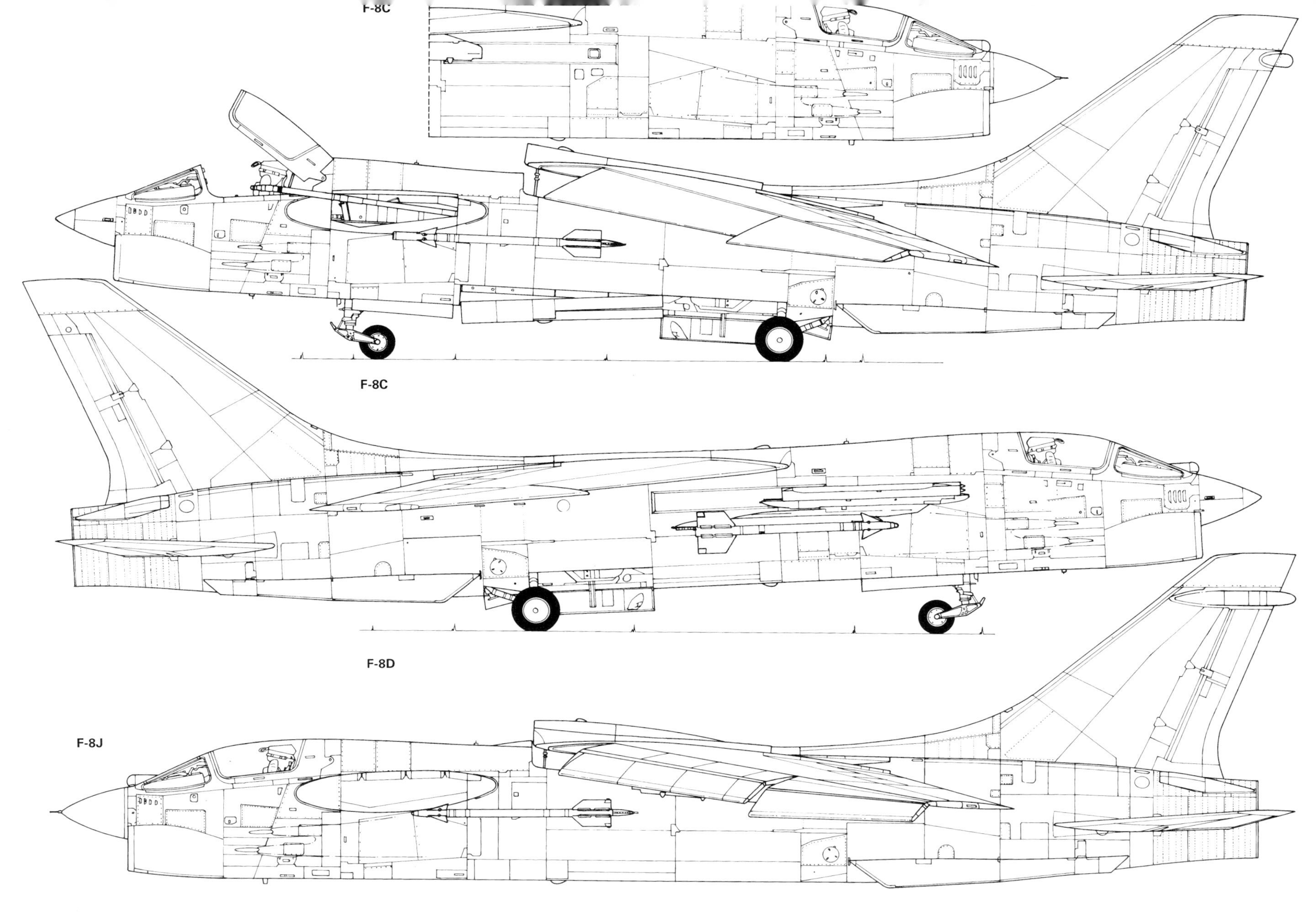
F-8C
F-8C
F-8D
F-8J

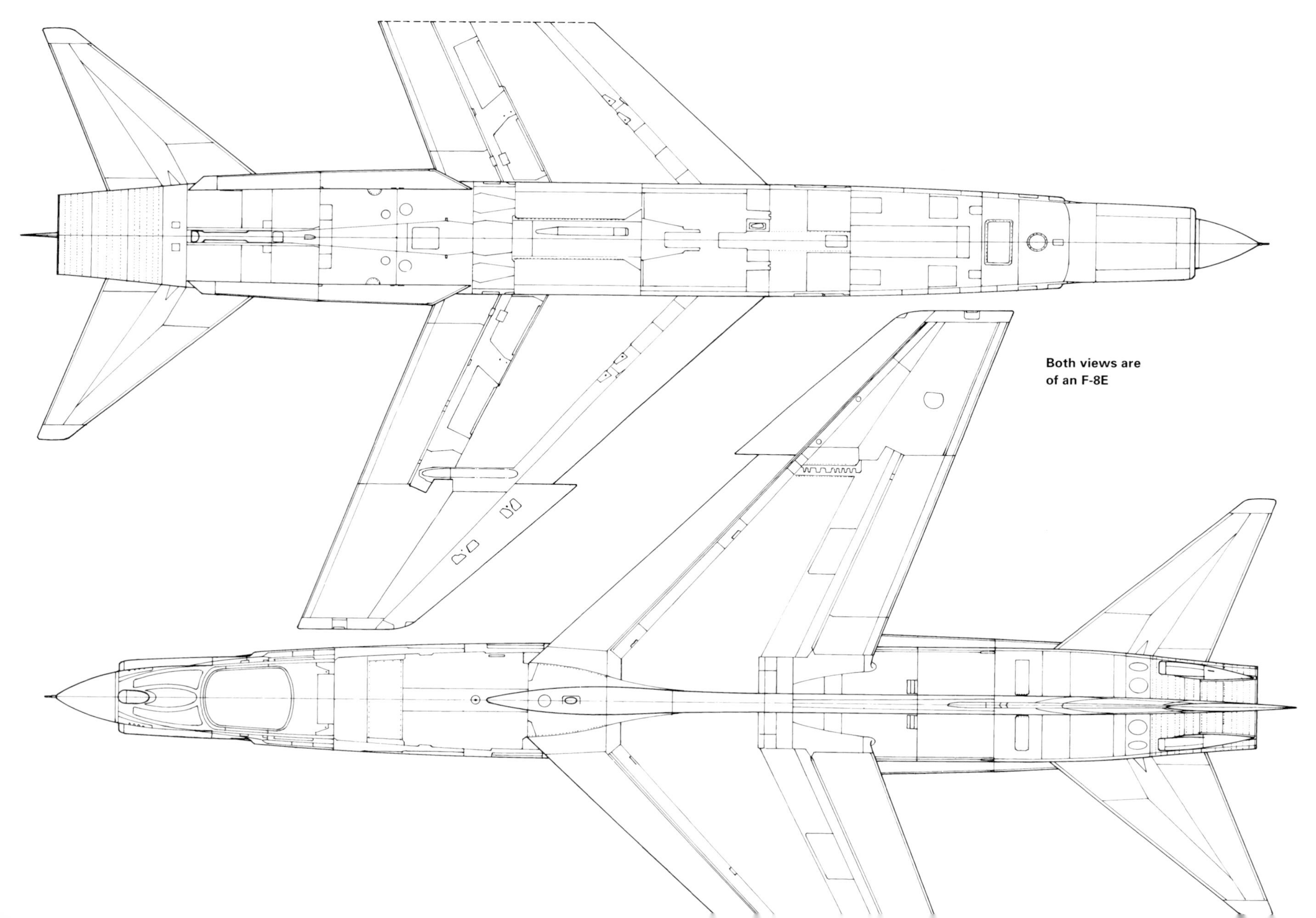
Both views are
of an F-8E

COLOUR PLATES

Note: Ticonderoga and Oriskany were battles fought during the 1777 New York campaign of the American Revolution. *Bon Homme Richard* was a French warship given to the American Navy and commanded by early US naval hero John Paul Jones in his famous battle with HMS *Serapis* in 1779. John Hancock was the first signer of the Declaration of Independence – he made his signature large and distinctive to make sure the British knew his name. 'Putting your "Hancock"' on a document subsequently became an American phrase for signing an official paper. In 1942, Coral Sea (May) and Midway (June) were pivotal naval engagements in the Pacific during World War 2.

1

F-8E BuNo 150924 NP 103 of Cdr Harold L Marr, CO of VF-211, USS *Hancock*, 12 June 1966

This F-8E was used by Cdr Marr to score the Crusader's premier combat kills – MiG-17s – on 12 June 1966. The aircraft was later shot down by flak on 6 October 1966 while serving as AH 201 of VF-162, its pilot, Lt R D Leach, being recovered.

2

F-8E BuNo 150300 NP 104 of Lt(jg) Phillip V Vampatella, VF-211, USS *Hancock*, 21 June 1966

Lt(jg) Vampatella was Hal Marr's wingman during the historic 21 June 1966 dogfight, scoring the second F-8 MiG kill achieved that day. He subsequently received the second Navy Cross awarded for aerial action in Vietnam in the wake of this mission. Vampatella's aircraft was also shot down by flak soon after the MiG action, being lost on 6 August 1966 again while serving with VF-162 – wearing the modex AH 211 at the time, the jet's pilot, Lt Cdr D A Verich, was recovered.

3

F-8E BuNo 149159 AH 210 of Cdr Richard M Bellinger, CO of VF-162, USS *Oriskany*, 9 October 1966

The legendary Dick Bellinger used this jet to score the Navy's first MiG-21 kill on 9 October 1966. Although wearing standard squadron markings, this aircraft did not carry the *Snoopy* drawing near the fin cap as seen on a number of other VF-162 aircraft during the cruise.

4

F-8E BuNo 150923 NP 110 of Lt Cdr Marshall O 'Mo' Wright, VF-211, USS *Bon Homme Richard*, 1 May 1967

'Mo' Wright's MiG-killing F-8E has often been given the modex 107, but the pilot emphatically reports that the correct number was 110, as seen here in this artwork. Later upgraded into an F-8J, the aircraft was shot down by flak on 20 June 1972 whilst still serving with VF-211. The pilot on its final mission was none other than squadron CO, Cdr Jim Davis, who was recovered.

5

F-8E BuNo 150661 NP 102 of Lt(jg) Joseph M Shea, VF-211, USS *Bon Homme Richard*, 19 May 1967

Normally assigned as Cdr Paul Speer's wingman, Lt(jg) Shea flew NP 102 on numerous occasions during the 1967 cruise, despite the fact that aircraft with the '02' modex usually carried the executive officer's name beneath the cockpit. He recalls that the painters in the squadron were kept busy moving side numbers around to ensure the best-looking aircraft were flown by the CO and his wingman! Thus, both Shea and his skipper, now-retired Rear Adm Speer, cannot remember with certainty which numbers they flew on their MiG-killing engagement. But both have reported usually flying NP 102 and NP 101, respectively.

6

F-8C BuNo 147029 NP 443 of Lt Phillip R Wood, VF-24, USS *Bon Homme Richard*, 19 May 1967

The subject of Iain Wyllie's cover artwork, this aircraft was flown by Lt Wood on his 19 May 1967 MiG-killing sortie. NP 443 was so badly damaged by cannonfire from a pursuing MiG-17 that after Wood recovered aboard USS *Kitty Hawk*, it was struck below decks and duly craned off in the Philippines, never to fly again.

7

F-8C BuNo 147018 NP 442 of Cdr Marion H 'Red' Isaacks, VF-24, USS *Bon Homme Richard*, 21 July 1967

This jet was used by VF-24's squadron executive officer, Cdr 'Red' Isaacks, to destroy a MiG-17 on 21 July 1967. This unit made nine combat deployments during the Vietnam War – eight in *Hancock* and one in *Bon Homme Richard* – and lost seven aircraft in action. The 'Checkertails' flew the Crusader until October 1975, when they transitioned to the F-14A Tomcat. The unit decommissioned in the 1990s in the flood of squadron 'deaths' due to the wave of downsizing that swept over the military establishments of many countries.

8

F-8E BuNo 150859 NP 107 of Lt Cdr Ray G 'Tim' Hubbard, VF-211, USS *Bon Homme Richard*, 21 July 1967

One of the most highly decorated F-8 'drivers' of the Vietnam War, 'Tim' Hubbard was amongst the handful of Crusader pilots who probably scored two MiG kills but never managed to get the second victory confirmed. His sole officially recognised kill (a MiG-17) was downed in this jet on 21 July 1967. Remanufactured as an F-8J sometime after completing its 1967 cruise, BuNo 150859 was subsequently lost in an operational mishap on 8 May 1970. VF-211's markings remained remarkably uniform throughout the Vietnam War, the ground crews maintaining the red-and-white checkerboard designs in relatively pristine condition even in the thick of combat operations.

9

F-8C BuNo 146992 NP 447 of Lt Cdr Robert L Kirkwood, VF-24, USS *Bon Homme Richard*, 21 July 1967

This jet was used by Lt Cdr Kirkwood to score the sole confirmed guns-only MiG kill credited to the F-8. Some confusion exists regarding the exact identity of this Crusader, as an end-of-cruise photo shows the F-8 at Miramar with its BuNo clearly displayed. However, the name on the canopy rail is that of Bobby Lee, who scored a kill on 19 May 1967 in F-8C 146981. While the side number and pilot name can, and did, change during a cruise, the BuNo remains constant. Of course it is entirely possible that Kirkwood flew this Crusader just as marked, with the name of another MiG killer from VF-24 worn on the canopy rail.

10

F-8E BuNo 150879 AH 204 of Lt Richard E Wyman, VF-162, USS *Oriskany*, 14 December 1967

Lt Wyman used this F-8E to down a MiG-17 with a Sidewinder after one of the war's longest aerial engagements on 14 December 1967. As with VF-211 (albeit for a shorter time), VF-162's markings remained constant during their war cruises with the F-8, the unit using the black-band-yellow-star motif designed by 1965 squadron member Bud Flagg. The only variable was the application of a missile-riding *Snoopy* from *Peanuts* just below the fin tip, this artwork being applied with the permission of cartoonist Charles Schultz, creator of the popular comic strip.

11

F-8H BuNo 148710 NL 116 of Lt Cdr Lowell R 'Moose' Meyers, VF-51, USS *Bon Homme Richard*, 26 June 1968

Although used by Lt Cdr 'Moose' Meyers to down his MiG-21 on 26 June 1968, this F-8H wore the name LTJG N.K. MCCOY on the canopy rails – the latter individual would score a kill six weeks later in BuNo 147916, NF 102 (see profile 14). Meyers' kill gave VF-51 victories in World War 2, Korea and Vietnam, and another four victories (all MiG-17s) would later be added by VF-51 crews flying the F-4B from *Coral Sea* in May/June 1972. Thus, long-time airwing partners VF-51 and VF-111 shared the unique claim of aerial kills in three major conflicts, as well as in the two main naval fighters in Vietnam (VF-111 also got a single MiG-17 kill in the F-4B during the 1972 *Coral Sea* cruise).

12

F-8E BuNo 150926 NM 101 of Lt Cdr John B Nichols III, VF-191, USS *Bon Homme Richard*, 9 July 1968

Lt Cdr Nichols III used this F-8E on 9 July 1968 to kill a MiG-17 which had made one of the few recorded direct attacks on an RF-8 whilst on a reconnaissance sortie over the north. Re-manufactured as an F-8J upon the completion of the 1968 cruise, BuNo 150926 was lost in an operational mishap while serving with VF-194 aboard *Oriskany* on 21 May 1969. Cdr Nichols went on to led VF-24 during the 1973 combat cruise aboard USS *Hancock*, and after retiring from the Navy, he co-wrote a novel – *The Warriors* – with well-known aviation writer and historian, Barrett Tillman (see *Osprey Combat Aircraft 3 - Helldiver Units of World War 2* for an example of the latter's work). The book dealt with a the conflict in the Middle East, ending in a nuclear attack by the Israel Air Force. Nichols and Tillman also co-wrote a history of the naval air war in Vietnam, titled *On Yankee Station*.

13

F-8E BuNo 150349 NF 203 of Lt Cdr Guy Cane, VF-53, USS *Bon Homme Richard*, 29 July 1968

Although often listed as a commander at the time of his MiG kill on 29 July 1968, Guy Cane (like Lt Cdr Meyers of VF-51) had only been *selected* for promotion – he eventually retired as a captain. The 'Iron Angels' continued flying the Crusader until they were decommissioned in January 1971.

14

F-8H BuNo 147916 NF 102 of Lt Norman K McCoy, VF-51, USS *Bon Homme Richard*, 1 August 1968

Recent information suggests that the pilot of the MiG-21 downed by Norm McCoy in this F-8H on 1 August 1968 was an eight-kill North Vietnamese ace. The latter individual survived his ejection and returned to his MiG-21 squadron, only to be killed in action on the morning of 10 May 1972 when his MiG was jumped and shot down by a VF-92 Phantom II crew (Lt Curt Dose and Lt Cdr James McDevitt in F-4J BuNo 157269 NG 211, launched from USS *Constellation*).

15

F-8C BuNo 146961 AK 103 of Lt Anthony J Nargi, VF-111, USS *Intrepid*, 9 September 1968

This aircraft was used by Lt Nargi to score the last confirmed F-8 kill of the war. Note the word *TIGER* (the call sign of Lt Joe Thompson) painted in white on the red tail band, and the red 'Omar' character above band – other call signs used during this cruise included 'Rattler' for Lt(jg) Alex Rucker and 'Roadrunner' for Lt Joe Satrapa. Lt(jg) Alex Rucker (Nargi's wingman) designed the slanting AK tail code worn by the F-8s allocated to Det 11/CVW-10 on this cruise. VF-111 flew C-, D-, E- and H-model Crusaders in combat over Vietnam.

16

F-8J BuNo 150900 NP 101 of Lt Jerry Tucker, VF-211, USS *Hancock*, 23 May 1972

This aircraft was Jerry Tucker's mount (although it was assigned to his CO, Cdr Jim Davis – see canopy rail) when he scored a much-discussed 'unofficial' kill on 23 May 1972, his 'victim' abandoning his MiG-17 *before* Tucker could fire a missile. Prior to this late-war cruise, BuNo 150900 had seen action both in 1965 as an E-model with VF-53 (wearing the modex NF 234 – see profile 32) aboard *Ticonderoga* and then (as NF 209 – see profile 33) aboard *Hancock* two years later.

17
F-8E BuNo 150654 WD 107 of VMF(AW)-212, USS *Oriskany*, 1965

The 'Lancers' were welcomed aboard *Oriskany* when they replaced the carrier's F-3 Demon squadron, VF-161 'Chargers' – the latter unit subsequently switched air wings to CVW-15 (and carriers to *Constellation*) following its transition from the Demon to the Phantom II in 1965-66. The Marines were among the first Crusader pilots to use the Mk 84 2000-lb bomb (a World War 2-vintage weapon, seen here affixed to the jet's wing pylon), thus demonstrating the F-8E's prodigious lifting ability. When Air Wing 16's leader, Cdr James Stockdale, was shot down in September 1965, the 'Lancers'' CO, Lt Col Charles Ludden, became the first Marine aviator to command a carrier air wing since World War 2.

18
F-8E BuNo 150675 DR 00 of VMF(AW)-312, assigned to Col R F Conley, MAG-11 CO, Da Nang, 1966

Col Conley was allocated this F-8E at NAS Atsugi, Japan, immediately prior to the unit's deployment to Da Nang, RVn, in December 1965. As a F3D pilot, Conley had scored one of the first night kills with a jet when he had downed a MiG-15 during the Korean War (see *Osprey Aircraft of the Aces 4 - Korean War Aces* for further details). His F-8E was among the most decorated Crusaders of the war period – note the Marine convention of a two-digit modex instead of the Navy-style three-number identification. VMF(AW)-312 was one of three Marine Corps F-8 fighter squadrons that deployed to Vietnam, although unlike the remaining two, it completed just one combat tour with the Crusader before transitioning to the F-4B Phantom II.

19
F-8E BuNo 150297 WT 3 of VMF(AW)-232, MAG-12, Da Nang, 1966

Amongst the oldest of all Marine Corps squadrons (one of the most active SBD units in World War 2, then designated VMSB-232 served with distinction at Guadalcanal and in subsequent campaigns in the Pacific), the 'Red Devils' became one of only two F-8 VMFs to return to Vietnam after transitioning to Phantom IIs. The unit also gained the dubious distinction of having suffered the only confirmed Marine loss to a North Vietnamese MiG when F-4J BuNo 155811 – crewed by Lts S G Cordova (MIA) and D L Borders (recovered) – was downed (allegedly by six-kill ace Lt Nguyen Duc Soat) on 26 August 1972.

20
F-8E BuNo 149204 DB 6 of VMF(AW)-235, MAG-12, Da Nang, 1967

VMF(AW)-235 was not only one of the most recognisable of all Crusader squadrons thanks to its adoption of a prominent red, star-spangled, nose marking (dubbed the 'Bozo Nose' after a populare television clown) and matching fin and ventral strakes, it was also the most active of the land-based 'Leatherneck' F-8 units. Perhaps as a result of their full schedule of combat missions, VMF(AW)-235's aircraft always seemed to be the most dirty F-8s in-theatre judging from contemporary colour photos taken at Da Nang in 1967-68 – their gun ports and fuselages were usually streaked with black grim, signifying much use. By the end of their final deployment in 1968, the 'Death Angels'' Crusaders had earned their rest. Although the squadron soon transitioned to the F-4J later that same year, it never returned to Vietnam.

21
DF-8D BuNo 143738 UE 1 of VC-5, Da Nang, 1965

These unusually-marked Crusaders towed targets and controlled drones from Da Nang and Chu Lai, Fleet Composite Squadron 5 flying examples of most Crusader variants until 1970. The unit remained in the Pacific as the area aggressor squadron, flying A-4Es from the Philippines (as well as SH-3D helicopters in the utility role), until disestablished in 1992.

22
F-8D BuNo 147908 NE 461 of VF-111, USS *Midway*, 1965

Using a relatively high modex number, this 'Delta' is finished in a typical VF-111 early-war scheme – simple red tail stripe, wingtips and ventral fin edge, and the sharkmouth intake marking, which was unique among Crusader squadrons. Compare this scheme with profiles 15 and 26, which show VF-111 F-8s wearing the same basic scheme, but with the addition of 'Sundowner' rudder flashes.

23
F-8D BuNo 148673 NL 413 of VF-154, USS *Coral Sea*, 1965

The 'Black Knights' flew many of the first raids against North Vietnam, losing six aircraft between 11 February and 14 October 1965. The penultimate Crusader classified as lost in combat was this 'Delta', which crashed on 9 May 1965, resulting in the death of its pilot, Lt D A Kardell. Despite rapidly transitioning to the F-4B soon after completing its initial war cruise, and subsequently making a further six combat deployments, VF-154 ended the conflict as one of the few VF squadrons that failed to get a MiG kill. Moving onto the F-14A in late 1983, the squadron still survives today as the sole Tomcat unit permanently assigned to AIRPAC, having been forward deployed with CVW-5 in Japan since 1991.

24
F-8C BuNo 146936 NP 450 flown by Lt(jg) Tom Irwin, VF-24, USS *Hancock*, February 1965

The markings worn by this F-8C are somewhat

subdued in comparison with later variations which adorned 'Checkertail' jets on subsequent cruises. Although US carrier air wings use sequential numbers for various squadrons, with fighter units being traditionally numbered in the 100 and 200 series, VF-24 and VF-111 used the 400 series, following their particular wings' A-4 light-attack squadrons. This variation occurred because one of the air wing's regular fighter units had transitioned to another type, being duly replaced by a different Crusader squadron. For example, *Hancock*'s F-3 Demon-equipped VF-213 changed to the F-4B, and was subsequently replaced by VF-24, which assumed the next available series – CVA-19's remaining fighter squadron, VF-211, kept its 100 series numbers. The sequence remained unchanged through to 1967, when the A-4 squadrons began to transition to A-7s.

25

F-8E BuNo 148178 NF 101 of Cdr James Stockdale, CO of VF-51, USS *Ticonderoga*, August 1964

This was the Crusader used by Cdr Stockdale during the first American strikes on North Vietnamese bases undertaken in the summer of 1964. Stockdale became one of the legendary characters of the war, suffering through eight years of hellish confinement and torture after being shot down and captured on 9 September 1965. He received the Medal of Honor for his determined leadership during this terrible period, eventually retiring as a vice admiral (three stars). However, when assigned F-8E NF 101, all this lay before him as he flashed low over the Communist shore facilities to avenge the PT-boat attacks on American destroyers.

26

F-8C BuNo 146999 AH 106 of Lt Cdr Dick Schaffert, VF-111, USS *Oriskany*, 14 December 1967

Lt Cdr Schaffert fought for his life in this F-8C during a frantic MiG engagement on 14 December 1967, the 'Sundowner' receiving a Distinguished Flying Cross for his determined defence of his A-4 flight against daunting odds. He later flew Phantom IIs before retiring with the rank of captain.

27

F-8J BuNo 149210 NP 112 of Lt Rick Amber, VF-211, USS *Hancock*, January 1971

A popular pilot amongst his air wing 'buddies', Lt Amber had completed half of CVW-21's 1971 combat deployment when he suffered a disastrous ramp strike and crash, which left him paralysed. Despite his physical disabilities, Rick Amber pursued a busy civilian career for which he was universally admired after being invalided out of the Navy. He died in 1997.

28

F-8J BuNo 149180 NM 103 of VF-191, USS *Oriskany*, 1975

The final cruise for the F-8, aboard *Oriskany*, ended disappointingly early due to a typhoon in South-East Asia, CVA-34 decommissioning soon after returning to San Diego in March 1976. VF-191 survived for another two years in Phantom IIs, but was eventually 'decommed' too in 1978. However, the squadron returned in F-14s for a brief period in 1986 as part of the reborn – more appropriately stillborn – Air Wing 10.

29

F-8J BuNo 150662 NM 204 of VF-194, USS *Oriskany*, 1975

Partnering VF-191 (as it had done for over a decade) on the Crusader's final cruise was VF-194. Like VF-154, the 'Red Lightnings' also failed to claim a MiG kill during the war. As with 'Satan's Kittens', VF-191 went to Phantom IIs in 1976 before being decommissioned in 1978, then reappearing with Tomcats for a short period eight years later.

30

F-8E BuNo 149199 NF 211 of Lt Jerry A Weber, VF-53, USS *Bon Homme Richard*, 1967

Flown by Lt Weber (who successfully made two ejections during the course of this deployment) on many missions during the 1967 cruise, this aircraft had also completed a previous tour with VF-211 as NP 100. Jerry Weber later served as a TAR (Training, Administration, Reserve) officer with VFP-306, flying RF-8Gs from NAF Washington in the 1970s. He retired as a captain.

31

F-8H BuNo 147908 NP 214 of VF-24, USS *Hancock*, 1969

This aircraft is unusual for it has VF-24's traditional chevron and 'checker' markings applied in yellow instead of red. For once the modex is correct, using the 200 series instead of the more familiar 400s as seen on other cruises. This particular cruise was undertaken in a period of relative inactivity over Vietnam, coming right after the far-reaching October 1968 bombing halt, which prohibited missions (except for unarmed reconnaissance flights) into North Vietnam, unless as a response to North Vietnamese attacks.

32

F-8E BuNo 150900 NF 234 of VF-53, USS *Ticonderoga*, 1965

A remarkably long-lived aircraft, especially for such a combat veteran F-8 (see profiles 16 and 33), BuNo 150900 flew early war cruises with VF-53 aboard *Ticonderoga*. During the 1965 deployment it undoubtedly participated in some of the conflict's first actions, including the series of engagements in the Gulf of Tonkin.

33

F-8E BuNo 150900 NF 209 of VF-53, USS *Hancock*, 1967

Renumbered NF 209, BuNo 150900 was aboard *Hancock* during the busy 1967 war cruise. After VF-53 decommissioned in 1971, the veteran 'Echo' was assigned to VF-211, where it earned its brief moment of fame as an unofficial MiG-killer (see profile 16).

FIGURE PLATES

1
Lt(jg) Phil Vampatella of VF-211, aboard USS *Hancock*, not only scored the second Navy MiG kill of the war in June 1966, but also earned the first Navy Cross awarded to a fighter pilot in Vietnam. In full flying kit, he displays his squadron patch and personal sidearm. Note the various leads for the helmet mike chord, and the standard practice of carrying the A-13A oxygen mask on the right harness strap through Velcro patch attachments. His upper torso harness also features rocket-jet fittings, these rather complex male-female devices connecting the harness to the ejection seat and parachute. They featured buttons on either side, which had to be squeezed simultaneously to release the pilot from his 'chute. By 1966 the rocket-jet fittings had begun being replaced by koch fittings, which required far less dexterity to disconnect, especially if the pilot was injured, or his hands were cold from exposure – a common concern when ejecting over water. Note the 'V' ring below the rocket-jet fitting on Vampatella's right shoulder. This design (the ring was a hoist connector) was replaced by the current oval ring.

2
Cdr James B Stockdale, CO of VF-51, sailing in USS *Ticonderoga*, led the first retaliatory strikes in August 1964. A year later, as air wing commander CVW-16 in USS *Oriskany* he was shot down in an A-4 and began eight years as a PoW. He received the Medal of Honor for his heroism during those years as a prisoner. Although the few photos taken during his combat tours show him in camouflaged fatigues, these were during his time as commander, CVW-16 on board *Oriskany*. Stockdale is wearing a standard issue one-piece khaki flying suit, over which he has strapped on an SV-2 survival vest, MA-2 torso harness, W/Mk-3C waist life-preserver and Mk-2 anti-gravity (G-suit).

3
Cdr Dick Bellinger, CO of VF-162 aboard USS *Oriskany* in October 1966. Amongst the most colourful of all F-8 'drivers', Bellinger was also one of the oldest fighter pilots to score a MiG kill, his victory being the first Navy success against the MiG-21. Tough, boisterous but a skilled aviator, Bellinger usually wore the camouflaged utilities, two-piece fatigues (not true flight suits) associated with several generations of early-war aviators. Over his utilities he is wearing the regulation Mk-2 anti-gravity (G-suit), MA-2 torso harness and a Mk-3C waist life-preserver. Definitely non-regulation are his two-toned jungle boots, worn in place of the aviator's steel-toed flight boots. Although most photos show Bellinger bare-headed, VF-162 pilots' helmets had a striking black-and-yellow-star design.

4
Lt Cdr Richard Schaffert of VF-111, aboard USS *Oriskany*, in December 1967. In what became one of the longest aerial engagements of the Vietnam War, Dick Schaffert fought a near-legendary one-man defence against a flight of aggressively flown MiG-17s attacking a group of A-4s. Representative of the early and mid-war group of tough, no-nonsense, Crusader 'drivers', Schaffert threw his fighter around the sky as he fended off several determined thrusts by the MiGs until help arrived. Even then, it took several engagements and several misguided Sidewinders before one MiG was downed by Dick Wyman. Note Schaffert's 35 mm camera, which naval aviators carried at the request of the ship's intelligence department. A few pilots took the intel officer's tasking seriously, but others merely shot off the roll when they got bored on usually quiet and unproductive CAP missions. Schaffert is cradling his large APH-6 flight helmet, APH standing for Aviator's Protective Helmet. By this time (1967) his torso harness had four koch fittings, although some aviators still wore suits with a combination of upper kochs and rocket jet fittings in the lap positions. By 1969 the transition to all-koch fittings was complete.

5
Capt Peter 'Drax' Williams of VMF(AW)-235 at Da Nang in 1968. While the Navy carrier-based Crusader 'drivers' got the MiGs, the shore-based Marine Corps F-8s 'kept the faith' with their 'grunt brothers', providing on-call close air support with 5-inch Zunis and huge 2000-lb Mk 84 iron bombs. Sporting a huge moustache, 'Drax' Williams was a member of what became the best-known Marine F-8 squadron in August 1967. He retired as a major general in 1997, being one of the last senior 'Leatherneck' Crusader aviators still on active duty. Wearing identical flying gear to his Navy brethren featured in these figure plates, 'Drax' Williams also has an issue angled flashlight hanging from his SV-2 survival vest

6
Lt Dudley Moore of VF-194 in a pre-deployment orange flight suit at NAS Miramar, California, between combat cruises aboard USS *Ticonderoga* in 1966-67. Note his high-top brown flight boots, shoulder holster and leg garters, or restraints, above and below his knees – a feature of the Martin-Baker seats used in the Vietnam-period F-8 and F-4. The white or blue colouring of these straps signified where the individual garter went. One of the first things a pilot did after positioning himself in his ejection seat – before connecting his four harness fittings to the seat – was to thread a long cloth-covered cable through the four restraints and plug the cable into the opposite, lower portion, of the metal seat. If he had to eject,

and a split-second before the seat actually began moving up the rails, the cable pulled the pilot's legs tight against the seat to prevent them from flailing during the ejection.

COLOUR SECTION

1
AH 232 gets last-minute attention from the flight-deck hook-up men. Other crewmen huddle between the bow cats in front of a VA-164 A-4E. Note the yellow bulkhead and squadron name on the raised wing. The high numbers came (so the story goes) because the air wing commander wanted to keep aircraft numbering consecutive for immediate recognition. Thus, on this cruise, while VMF(AW)-212 carried the 100 series to 112, VF-162 started with the next, 213, instead of 201, 202, etc. It was another variation of the early-war numbering systems (*Rick Adams*)

2
The director beckons the pilot of AH 200 onto the catapult. Every squadron has an aircraft assigned to the air wing commander. A feature of this special aircraft's markings was the inclusion of all the wing colours, as on the black rudder. VF-162's black-band-and-yellow-star design was the work of Lt Bud Flagg. He also wrote to cartoonist Charles Schultz for permission to use the *Peanuts* character *Snoopy* on a Sidewinder. An Army veteran of World War 2, Schultz readily agreed (*Rick Adams*)

3
A good overhead view of AH 225 with a load of Zunis. The discoloration on the left wing is not corrosion, but rather a corrosion preventative applied in the hope that the deterioration hasn't already begun. It was later removed when more in-depth procedures could be accomplished. For the most part, however, anti-corrosion measures were at best a delaying tactic, but usually a losing battle (*Rick Adams*)

4
An F-8D of VF-111 is seen aboard USS *Midway* in 1965

5
VF-111 had an eventful 1966 cruise onboard USS *Oriskany*. As the 'shooter' touches the deck, this 'Sundowner' Crusader is ready to go flying for visiting Secretary for Defense Robert McNamara. Two weeks later, the flightdeck would be engulfed in smoke and flames in the horrific shipboard fire that struck CVA-34 on 26 October

6
Taken right after he returned from his successful MiG engagement, Lt Cdr Kirkwood is all smiles in his squadron's paraloft

7
Looking every inch the tough, bulky, fighter pilot that he was, Cdr Bellinger gets out of his F-8E after a mission in September 1966. Like many aviators of the period and locale, he wears two-piece camouflaged fatigues obtained from the Army

8
Lt Moore back at Miramar after the 1967 cruise. His orange flight suit was strictly for peacetime operations only

9
An F-8E of VMF(AW)-235 displays its colourful markings and a considerable load of ordnance, including Zuni rockets and iron bombs. This aircraft has obviously seen much combat, as evidenced by its blackened gun ports and dirty lower fuselage. Behind the Crusader is Da Nang's crowded flightline, with tails of EF-10s and F-4s visible. An A-6 is immediately to the right (in the photo)

10A and B
A green MiG-17 cuts across the North Vietnamese countryside during the epic encounter of 14 December 1967. One of a flight of four, the MiG was finally shot down by Lt Wyman of VF-162

11
Lt Nargi's F-8 MiG killer is seen on the cat

12
Lt Flagg poses by a Mk 84 bomb during the 1965 cruise

13
A 'Superheat' F-8E is seen during a CAP mission

14
Crewmen man-handle a VF-111 F-8D aboard USS *Midway* in the summer of 1965 (*NMNA*)

15
This VF-51 F-8H is positioned on *Bonnie Dick*'s waist cat ready for launch

16
Coming aboard. An F-8J of VF-24 heads for *Hancock*'s flightdeck during 1971 work-ups

17
The last cruise for fighter Crusaders. The *Oriskany* launches an F-8J in 1975. RF-8Gs of VFP-63 would continue to deploy for seven more years

18
Carrying yellow markings, instead of the traditional red, this VF-24 'Hotel' is seen on the *Hancock* in 1969

19
USS *Bon Homme Richard* leaves Pearl Harbor for a tour on 'Yankee Station' as sailors man the rails in their whites